TOWN·AND·CITY·GUIDES

AA

DUBLIN

TOWN·AND·CITY·GUIDES

The all-in-one guide to what goes on in and around the city

*Tourist information,
maps, walks, drives,
eating out, where to stay*

Produced by the Publishing Division of the Automobile Association

Cover picture: Trinity College

Title page: Dublin's coat of arms

Introductory pages: Street lamps in Dublin

Editor: Antonia Hebbert
Copy Editor: Sally Knowles

Art Editor: Dave Austin
Design Assistant: Neil Roebuck

Original Photography: George Munday, The Slide File
Additional photography: Jamie Blandford
Picture Research: Wyn Voysey

Editorial contributors: Pat Liddy (walks); Adrian MacLoughlin
(City Centre, Out of City); Séamus MacMathúna (Traditional
Music); Éamonn MacThomáis (Introduction, City Crafts); Charles
Nelson (Gardens of Dublin County); David Norris (Georgian
Houses, Literary Dublin); Kathy Sheridan (Directory); Peter
Somerville-Large (A Thousand Years and More).

The assistance of Dublin & East Tourism and Bord Fáilte is
gratefully acknowledged.

Maps and plans produced by the Cartographic Department of the
Automobile Association. Atlas based on Ordnance Survey
mapping and reproduced with the permission of the Ordnance
Survey of the Republic of Ireland (permit no 4001) and the
Ordnance Survey of Northern Ireland.

Filmset by Vantage Photosetting Co Ltd, Eastleigh and London,
England

Printed and bound by Graficromo SA, Spain

Produced and distributed in the United Kingdom by the
Publishing Division of the Automobile Association, Fanum
House, Basingstoke, Hampshire, RG21 2EA.

ISBN 0 86145 652 1

AA Reference 50717

CONTENTS

Introduction

The old black iron fender which guarded our Anna Liffey model range fireplace summed up Dublin for me in three words . . . . . 'Home Sweet Home'. Those three words were cut out like a stencil, and when the Mother used the Zebra black-lead polish on the hearth, they seemed to be made of ebony.

Dublin is a city of threes. It has three castles on its coat of arms, and it has three Gaelic names. Dubhlinne, the black or the dark river pool. Baile Atha Cliath, Baile the town and Atha Cliath the hurdle ford. And Druim Cuill Coillte—Druim the ridge and Cuill Coillte the hazel wood.

When the late Brendan Behan was singing about 'The Auld Triangle that went jingle jangle, Along the banks of the Royal Canal,' he was, without realising it, singing about some of the symbols of Dublin. My triangle of Dublin is like the spire of a church, with the high mountain tops running down one side and the golden sandy beaches and the coastline running down the other side. In the centre of the triangle is the valley, with the city, the people and the lights.

The three sides of the people of Dublin are friendship, good humour and colourful speech. Dubliners love visitors, because visitors ask questions and Dubliners love talking. Brendan Behan used to say that Dubliners spend words like sailors. Another good point about true Dubliners is that if they don't know the answer to your question, they will stop someone else to ask it, and then repeat the answer to you adding their little comment in their own special flavour and colour.

Dublin is a warm city. It has a triangle of colours, Georgian russet red, battleship grey and Liffey green. These colours are on its courts, churches, and the Custom House with its long room and its statue of Lady Hope looking down the River Liffey as it flows in and out of Dublin Bay.

When it comes to shopping, we have a triangle of ancient towns within the heart of the city. The main shopping area of Dublin has long been our Down Town Saturday night district, where we 'clicked the mots' (checked out the girls) and treated them to creamy coffee and sticky buns. Down Town O'Connell Street, the widest street in Europe, has a network of nine side streets and four quayside ways, all of them leading to glamour, excitement, bargains, fashions, music, cinemas, dancing, pubs, coffee shops and fine restaurants. One side street leads to the Abbey Theatre, which takes its name from the street itself. Another leads to Mary Street, where James Joyce opened the first cinema in Ireland, the Volta, at No 45.

The second shopping town—'let's try George's Street,' was the cry—is entered by the Halfpenny Bridge Gateway. Go under the Merchants Arch into Temple Bar, down by Crown Alley and out by the Central Bank Plaza into Dame Street and around the corner into George's Street.

South Great George's Street has the beautiful red brick South City Market, yet another gateway to the magic of the side streets. Adjoining Aungier Street leads to the Carmelite Church with its statues of St Jude, St Valentine, and the Black Madonna, Our Lady of Dublin.

The third shopping town to complete the triangle is the area of the ancient Liberties, so-called because they were outside old Dublin's jurisdiction. Each had its own court—the Liberty of Thomas Court and Donore, named after Thomas Becket, murdered in Canterbury Cathedral, the Liberty of the Archbishop of St Sepulchre, the Liberty of the Dean and Chapter of St Patrick's Cathedral and the Liberty of Christ Church Cathedral, the Liberty of St John outside Newgate and the Lord Mayor's Liberty inside the walls of Dublin. The Liberties is the spot for the bargains, the street sellers, the markets, the wit, the colour, the song, the 'crack', the real 'heart of the rowl' of Dublin City. How do you get there? Very simple! Stand with your back to Trinity College and follow your nose in a straight line. On the way you will pass City Hall, Dublin Castle, Christ Church Cathedral, St Audeons and the Tailors' Hall, the oldest guildhall in Dublin.

Trinity College leads to the glamour of Grafton Street which in the old days was very quiet, but now has been turned into another wonderful shopping town, leading to the Powerscourt Townhouse Centre and St Stephen's Green, where children feed the ducks or catch 'pinkeens' (little fish).

Outside the city are mountains

with primroses and cromlechs. When we were young we used to head for the Three-Rock Mountain, otherwise known as Slieve Rua, the 'red mountain'. We were never short of a mountain to explore—Kilmashogue, Tibradden, Glendoo Mountain across Glencullen Valley, Cruagh, Kilakee, and Mont Pelier, each of them with ghosts, leprachauns, wild flowers, green ferns, sparkling streams and a magnificent view of the city and the bay.

An easier way to have the whole of Dublin Bay before you is to travel by DART—Dublin Area Rapid Transit. North to Howth Head and the Marina Village, south to Bray Head and the

seaside towns of County Wicklow, this new railway with its trim green trains has won the hearts of Dubliners.

Dublin is a city to enjoy, where there is always something to do or some place to go . . . . the Phoenix Park, the National Gallery, the treasures of the Irish Nation in the National Museum. Or a picnic in the mountains, or merely a walk through the streets smelling the yeast and the hops up around St James's Gate Brewery, or the combined scents of Moore Street with its flowers, fruit, vegetables and meats, or Bewley's shops when they grind and brew the coffee . . .

This is Dublin—home sweet home.

ÉAMONN MACTHOMÁIS

About This Book

Dublin City Guide,
designed to be the complete guide for tourist or resident,
contains the following sections.

Features
Written by local experts, these introductory articles cover
subjects of special importance in the city—its literary
connections, its remarkable Georgian architecture, its long
tradition of craftsmanship and over a thousand years of history.
Also covered in this section are traditional Irish music, which
can be heard at numerous places in the city, and gardens to visit
both in Dublin and in the surrounding countryside.

City Centre: Places to Visit
Here places of interest, listed alphabetically, are described in
detail. Each entry includes its street name, so it can easily be
located on the street plan on page 102. For opening times and
practical information refer to the Directory.

City Walks
Six walks, with step-by-step route directions, have been
carefully planned to take in the best of the city. A clear, easy-to-
follow map accompanies each walk. The chief places of interest
along the way are described in the text, and these are keyed to
the maps by numbers.

Out of City: Places to Visit
An alphabetical selection of the most interesting places to visit
in the surrounding area. All within an hour or so's drive. For
opening times etc refer to the relevant section of the Directory.
Each entry has a grid reference, and can be located on the maps
on pages 96 to 99.

Day Drives
Two routes for exploring the countryside around the city,
including detailed route directions, a map and places of
interest.

District Maps
Four pages of mapping at a scale of 4 miles to the inch,
covering the area around the city, extending over 50 miles from
the city centre.

Through Routes
This shows the main roads in and out of the city.

City Plan
Large-scale map of the City Centre, with a street index and
places of interest clearly shown.

Directory
Twelve pages packed with useful information grouped into
sections (see page 104). All you need to know about where to
eat and stay, recreation, shops, sports and services, plus useful
addresses and opening times for all the places of interest
described in the book. A calendar of events lists the major
annual festivals, shows and sporting events month by month.

FEATURES

AA

TOWN·AND·CITY·GUIDES

A Dublin door: in this city of harmonious Georgian terraces, the different styles of fanlights, door cases and wrought iron railings are especially pleasing

A Thousand Years & More

Dublin, originally an ecclesiastical settlement, and then in turn a Viking raiding and trading base, a Norman stronghold, the British Empire's second city and capital of an independent state, is steeped in tragic and glorious history.

Dublin is generally considered a Viking creation – a Norse community older than Oslo or Bergen. But long before the arrival of the Vikings, people lived around the protected waters of Dublin Bay. Here Larnian hunters and fishermen kept dogs as domestic animals 5,000 years ago, and ate ox, sheep and pigs. Neolithic farmers built their tombs at the foot of the Dublin mountains, and a community of Beaker Folk (called after their pottery) flourished in the Bronze Age.

With the coming of Christianity a spread of monasteries and hermit cells appeared north and south of the Liffey. Along the Poddle, the Liffey's tributary, stood four churches, St Patrick on its island, St Brigid, St Kevin and St MacTaill, which are assumed to be Celtic foundations. The original small settlement was named Ath Cliath, 'ford of hurdles' and was at a cross-roads. Below the steep ridge on which stood the Church of St Columcille, later replaced by St Audeon, the Poddle met the Liffey, forming a pool – Linn Dubh, the Black Pool.

Vikings had been plundering the east coast of Ireland for decades. Then in the summer of AD837, 65 longboats sailed down from Scotland and Orkney. The traditional site of their Dublin has been confirmed by archaeology. Excavations around Christ Church have revealed the remains of post and wattle houses, and the detritus of the new town: fragments of Viking clothes and jewellery, bones of eaten animals, combs in their hundreds. The Battle of Dublin in December AD919 ensured the Viking settlement. Ireland temporarily united against the Vikings in the 11th century, who were routed at Clontarf in the greatest battle in early Irish history, on Good Friday, 23 April 1014.

Political unity did not last however, and appeals were made to Henry II of England for help. Thus began the Norman invasion of Ireland which culminated in Henry II's landing in 1171 and his assumption for the English crown of the Lordship of Ireland. He kept Dublin and its environs – the Pale – for himself.

The Normans were great builders. Apart from what survives in stone, part of the city wall, the cathedrals of St Patrick and Christ Church, Dublin Castle, the grim seat of government, and various churches and tombs, the most vivid reminders of the Norman presence are surviving street names: Bull Alley, Golden Lane, Cornmarket, High Street, Winetavern Street, Fishamble Street.

In spite of raids from Irishmen in the surrounding hills, a failed attempt to create a Celtic kingdom, siege, fire, and pestilence as the Black Death brought its devastation, medieval Dublin enlarged and grew more prosperous. A line of 12th-century warehouses excavated at Wood Quay indicates the importance of trade with Europe. Surviving assembly rolls and guild charters, descriptions of religious festivals, guild ceremonies and other events give clues to the life of the city. The new merchant class flourished, while the records of the Priory of the Holy Trinity provide evidence of a comfortable lifestyle for clergy and monks.

Silken Thomas's rebellion in 1534 heralded the demise of medieval Dublin. In the period between the accession of Henry VIII as King of Ireland in 1536, and the death of Queen Elizabeth in 1601, the

Reformation made its impact on the city, while the savage surrounding conflict, culminating in the defeat of Gaelic Ireland, strengthened the capital which became the main base of English operations against the Irish. The wave of new English settlers encouraged the impact of the Renaissance, and Trinity College, a counterblast to Popery, was founded in 1592 on land confiscated from All Hallows.

In the early part of the following century, dissent and civil war shrivelled Dublin to a wretched state. But after the constraints of the Commonwealth came the Restoration and Ormonde's viceroyalty, bringing increased trade. The city underwent a great architectural expansion. With a rising population, houses began to spill out beyond the old confines. By the end of the 17th century, Dublin was a flourishing commercial centre. During the following century it was transformed into one of the handsomest of Georgian cities, so that today it is hard for the visitor to ignore the influence of the 18th century. The beautiful rose-coloured brick terraces, elegant mansions, wide streets and squares made up one of Europe's finest capitals. But the century of Dean Swift, Lord Charlemont, Sheridan and the rest, was also a period of political agitation when the sufferings of the poor provided a perpetual contrast. In Malton's *Picturesque and Descriptive Views of the City of Dublin*, a beggar is usually present.

The age of elegance was brought to an end by a wave of political unrest, which erupted in the uprising by the United Irishmen in 1798. The rebellion was crushed by English armies, the Act of Union was established, and the fortunes of the city began to wane. During the 19th century the railway took over from the canal and the first horsedrawn tram made its way down Sackville Street. It was an age of great upheaval, with Daniel O'Connell's massive meetings inspiring cries for Repeal, and Parnell and Davitt fuelling the campaign for Home Rule. Catholic emancipation in 1829, by which

time Catholics formed over 70 per cent of the population, helped the rise of a new professional class. But poverty was also increasing, and the Dublin slums were reputed to be the worst in Europe.

A revival of interest in the Irish language and traditional Irish life, resulting in the formation of the Abbey Theatre in Dublin in 1904, heralded a remarkable literary age whose luminaries were Yeats, Synge, George (Æ) Russell and George Moore. Abroad in self-imposed exile, James Joyce created a giant record of his birthplace.

The end of the old order began with the Easter Rising of 1916 which was fought in Dublin's streets, bringing more fire and destruction to the city. When Civil War broke out in June 1922, shelling destroyed much of O'Connell Street, but the GPO and other buildings were later restored.

The Dublin that slowly emerged from the ashes of conflict touches our own age. Only a proportion of the elegant Georgian buildings survive, but much of the warm intimacy of Dublin life seems to survive in its spacious streets and handsome squares, as Dublin enters a new era.

CIVIL WAR
In 1922 the Four Courts was seized by those opposed to the new Free State Government

PARNELL
Charles Stewart Parnell, the 19th-century Home Rule campaigner

PETER SOMERVILLE-LARGE

Peter Somerville-Large is related to Edith Somerville of the Irish RM stories and has written several books on Ireland.

Georgian Houses

W ide, spacious streets and harmonious Georgian terraces
make Dublin one of Europe's most beautiful cities. A close
look at the terrace façades reveals a wealth of decorative detail, in
fanlights, door knockers and even coal hole covers, while within
are nobly proportioned rooms and gloriously exuberant
plasterwork.

PUBLIC BUILDINGS

The 18th century saw a flowering of splendid architecture, both for domestic and public structures. One of Dublin's finest public buildings is the Parliament House, with its monumental, colonnaded, windowless façade. It is now the headquarters of the Bank of Ireland

Dublin enjoys a superb natural location sheltered by the Dublin Mountains, watered by the River Liffey, the arms of the Bay reaching out as if in welcome to the traveller, so that it is not surprising that for a thousand years and more it has been a major centre of habitation. Little trace however of its medieval origin remains, apart from the line of some of the oldest streets and the two great cathedrals, Christ Church and St Patrick's (and even St Patrick's derives its principal international celebrity from association with the iconoclastic 18th-century writer Dean Jonathan Swift). To most people the essential spirit of Dublin, especially as expressed in architecture, is that of the 18th century. During that period Dublin, although governed as was the rest of the island by a Protestant Ascendancy, was the seat of an independent parliament under the British crown, second city of what was fast becoming an empire and the self-styled seventh city of Christendom. The confidence of the age is reflected in the great public buildings created by the genius of architects like James Gandon,

Thomas Ivory and Francis Johnston. Dublin's skyline is still dominated by such impressive works as the Royal Hospital Kilmainham, now magnificently restored, the Bluecoat School, the façade of Trinity College, the Custom House, the Four Courts, the Parliament House (now the Bank of Ireland, College Green) and the King's Inns in Henrietta Street. Apart from these magnificent places of public and professional resort, the domestic buildings of Georgian Dublin continued into the private sphere the ideals of harmony and balance, regularity and symmetry so dear to 18th-century classicism.

WIDE AND CONVENIENT STREETS

Nor was the coherent development of the capital left to the whim of individual taste, and Dubliners still have cause to be grateful to the 'Commissioners for Making Wide and Convenient Streets', known popularly as the Wide Street Commissioners. This influential body was established by an Act of 1757 and given the power to acquire and demolish unsatisfactory, dilapidated or inconvenient buildings, and to lay down strict standards governing the architectural character of new buildings which replaced them. They were also empowered to compensate individual builders for any additional expense incurred in meeting these standards. Among the streets to benefit from their attentions were Lower Sackville (now O'Connell) Street, Westmoreland Street, D'Olier Street, Dame Street and Rutland (now Parnell) Square. In 1773 a parallel body, the Paving Board, was set up to oversee the 'paving cleansing lighting draining and improving' of the city's streets. By the last quarter of the 18th century, Dublin was what Paris was to become only later under Napoleon, an elegant city of planned and luxuriously broad thoroughfares.

It was a compact city of less than 200,000 souls, lying entirely between the two canals – the Grand to the south of the city with its graceful locks and bridges such as the Huband Bridge (1791) at Percy Place, and the plainer, more straightforward Royal Canal on the north side. Indeed the keen observer can still clearly note the limits of the Georgian city in the stylistic change that occurs as the tidemark of Victoriana washes against it. The contrast between the mellow, honey-tinged Georgian brick and its heavier, more aggressively red Victorian counterpart is quite marked at points such as the junction of Belvedere Place and the North Circular Road on the north side, or at the meeting of Lower Mount Street and Northumberland Road on the south. It must be acknowledged however that Mount Street has now been almost totally destroyed and its original buildings recently replaced by high and unimaginative office blocks, while many of the imposing Victorian residences of Northumberland Road have completed the initial stages of transition to the commercial sector.

FROZEN IN TIME

Within its two canals central Dublin remained frozen in time, an almost totally intact Georgian anachronism until a sudden boom in property speculation in the early 1960s led to an unexpected and unparalleled devastation. Shamefully the signal for destruction was first given by a State agency – the Electricity Supply Board – which despite public protest pulled down 26 Georgian houses and set in their place a jarring modern office block, effectively destroying what had been the longest continuous Georgian vista in Europe – the view from Holles Street past Merrion Square and Fitzwilliam Square to the Dublin Mountains. In fact by the mid-1960s the core of Dublin had become vulnerable for a variety of reasons. The great houses of the nobility, set in splendid isolation like Leinster, Tyrone, Aldborough, Powerscourt and Charlemont Houses, or

in serried ranks along the streets and squares of the inner city, had been rapidly drained of their aristocratic occupants with the passing of the Act of Union in 1800, which abolished the independent Dublin Parliament. Throughout the 19th century the glory of the old mansions faded as they passed from the aristocracy into the hands of first the professional classes, then to merchants and tradespeople and ultimately to subdivision into tenements. This situation was compounded with the freezing of tenement rents during World War I, to avoid mutinous murmurings from the families of those at the front, and the problem thus created was left unresolved for 60 years after the war's end. This meant that rents became so uneconomic that non-resident landlords either refused or could not afford to carry out essential repairs. In addition, many officials of the New State established at the beginning of the 1920s felt alienated from this part of their heritage, seeing in Georgian Dublin merely the expendable remnant of an arrogant, exploitative and alien ruling class. Nowadays, happily, this phase has passed and the preservation of the best of what remains of Georgian Dublin is supported by all sectors, who appreciate that what is valued is not the pretensions of the past but the surviving work of Irish artists, craftsmen builders and 'stuccodores' – men like Charles Thorp, Francis Ryan, Michael Stapleton and Robert West.

GEORGIAN TOWN HOUSES

The typical pattern of the Georgian town house is that of a red brick, four-storey over basement construction, with a pitched and slated roof, granite steps to the hall door and a basement area protected by wrought or cast iron railings. An attractive feature of these houses was the division of the windows into small squares by glazing bars, and the delicately graceful leaded fanlights over the hall door, although sadly these have both been replaced over

DOORS
Door cases, fanlights and even foot scrapers give subtle variety to Georgian façades. Changes of use have lost No 48 its fanlight but gained it doctors' doorplates

AROUND THE STREETS

A favourite pastime of Dublin antiquarians is 'ceiling spotting'. This is best done at dusk when the lights are on in the first floor reception rooms, and the stroller can enjoy from a safe vantage point on the pavement the tracery of 18th-century plasterwork, often picked out in delicate pastel shades. The area around Merrion Square, Fitzwilliam Square and St Stephen's Green is a particularly rich location for this hobby. The squares themselves were originally for the private enjoyment of the residents, but in St Stephen's Green, Merrion Square and Mountjoy Square, Dublin Corporation Parks Department now maintain well-tended public pleasure gardens. The most recently opened of these, Merrion Square, is a particular delight in which it is possible to refresh the weary spirit in the mellow ambience of the past and relish the full impact of the surrounding buildings away from the roar of the traffic. Number 63 Merrion Square, finely restored, is the headquarters of the Irish Architectural Archive and houses a unique collection of photographs, plans and architectural drawings.

Although there is now considerable modern intrusion into St Stephen's Green, some fine 18th-century houses do remain, notably No 86, originally the home of Burnchapel Whaley and his son Buck Whaley who won a bet by walking to Jerusalem and playing handball against its walls. This subsequently became part of University College Dublin, and the setting for a number of celebrated scenes in the novels of James Joyce, its most distinguished graduate. Number 85 next door has a very fine ceiling in the saloon by Francini. On the same side is the imposing Iveagh House, remodelled by Sir Benjamin Guinness and presented to the nation by the 2nd Earl of Iveagh, also a member of the brewing family, in 1939. It now houses the Department of Foreign Affairs and provides a glorious background for state dinners.

Just off the Green are three superb

DOOR DETAILS
The observant person, walking round the streets of Dublin, will have fun spotting door decorations such as window grills, letter boxes and Georgian door knockers

PLASTERWORK
Ceiling in Dominick Street (opposite) and detail (right): the glory of Dublin's town houses lies in their plasterwork decoration. Great 'stuccodores' (plaster-workers), like Robert West and Michael Stapleton, modelled the wet plaster on the ceiling itself (and on friezes and walls). Later plasterwork was made in moulds

the years in some houses by plain glass. The apparent uniformity of the brick façade and the regularity of the roofline in a streetscape can mislead the casual observer into ignoring the subtle variation in detail. There is in fact a surprising variety of door cases, and the sharp eyed will enjoy the range of imagination displayed in items such as door knockers in the guise of human heads or animal forms, the differing shapes of foot scrapers, the individualistic patterns of leaves, spirals or geometrical arabesques decorating even the humble cast iron coal hole covers inserted into the granite paving sets. Here and there on the railings can be found the remains of the standard brackets which once held candle- or oil-lit lanterns, a relic of the 17th-century ordinance under which every fifth house was obliged to provide lighting for the public footpath.

The real magnificence of these houses only becomes apparent when one penetrates behind the somewhat restrained façades. The noble proportions of high-ceilinged rooms are pleasing in themselves, but the great glory of Dublin lies in the unique lightness and exuberance of the plasterwork decoration on ceilings, friezes and walls. A small number of private houses are open to the public on a limited basis and a list of these may be obtained from the offices of Dublin Tourism in O'Connell Street.

of Viscount Powerscourt. It has now been
brought back to life as an up-market
shopping and restaurant complex. Visitors
have free access to the interior which has a
large number of fine rooms, richly
decorated with plasterwork by James
McCullagh and Michael Stapleton, as well
as an elaborately carved wooden staircase
by Ignatius McDonagh. Probably the
grandest house still in private occupation
as a family residence is No 1 Grafton
Street, the Provost's House, home of the
Provost of Trinity College. The saloon,
with its splendid, coved ceiling, runs the
entire length of the building.

The north side of Dublin, originally the
most fashionable sector, has suffered
greatly over the years, but there are even
here some remarkable pockets of survival.
Henrietta Street, although sadly
dilapidated, contains some of the most
palatial and beautifully decorated houses in
Dublin, and as a result of the dedicated
work of a handful of restorationists, is
undergoing a slow and painful process of
recuperation. Closer to O'Connell Street is
Dominick Street, where only a tiny cluster
of houses remains at the top end. Luckily a
number of these are quite spectacular,
notably No 20 (now an orphanage), the
masterwork of the stuccodore Robert
West whose high relief plaster birds seem
to start from the plane surfaces as if about
to fly away. Between Dominick Street and
O'Connell Street lies Parnell Square, now
considerably defaced but retaining some
very good buildings, the most notable of
which are Charlemont House (now the
Municipal Gallery), and the Rotunda
Hospital complex, Europe's first lying-in
hospital, whose chapel boasts
appropriately exuberant and joyful
baroque plasterwork featuring cherubs
emerging into life from walls and ceiling.

UNEXPECTED BEAUTIES

Parallel to Parnell Square is North Great
George's Street, the sister street to
Dominick Street, but unlike it almost
totally intact and largely in residential
ownership. An anonymous English
traveller writing in 1917 in a book called
Dublin Explorations and Reflections wrote –
'North Great George's Street, though at
first glance of comparatively modest
appearance, is really one of the finest
streets in the whole of Dublin. Some of the
empty houses, which I used to amuse
myself by going over, almost took one's
breath away their beauties were so
unexpected.' They were built during the
most brilliant period of the Ascendancy,
and the interior plasterwork in the houses
is by the greatest of the Irish craftsmen,
Michael Stapleton, Francis Ryan and
Charles Thorp among others, and ranges
from rococo, with gothic coved entrance
halls and trophies of birds and fruit
decorating the friezes, to a more classical
Adam-influenced style. Fanlights, foot
scrapers and glazing bars have survived
here as has an occasional lamp standard set
on the railings. The elaborate doorcase of

houses: Ely House, Northland House and
Powerscourt House. Ely House is in Ely
Place facing down Hume Street towards
the Green. The plasterwork here is by
Michael Stapleton, and one of the unusual
features of the house is a beautiful
wrought iron staircase with panels
depicting the labours of Hercules. At the
beginning of the century this was the
residence of the surgeon Sir Thornley
Stoker, brother of Bram Stoker, author of
Dracula. It is now the headquarters of the
Knights of Columbanus, a conservative
Roman Catholic organisation. Northland
House, No 19 Dawson Street, has been the
home of the Royal Irish Academy since the
middle of the last century, and is
remarkable for its rococo plasterwork in
the so-called 'Chinese taste', white on a
green ground. Powerscourt House, in
South William Street just behind Grafton
Street, was built in 1771 as the town house

No 38, former home of Oscar Wilde's tutor Rev Sir John Pentland Mahaffy, is one of the finest in Dublin. The Loreto Convent in the middle of the street possesses one of the few remaining original Bossi fireplaces. Once a feature of great Dublin houses, these slender, elegant creations were of white marble inset with coloured stone to represent fruit, garlands or classical scenes. Crowning the street is Belvedere House, now a Jesuit College and one of the city's most splendid 18th-century mansions. The staircase here is so encrusted with plasterwork, again by Stapleton, that it has raised the fastidious disdain of some purists, but to the less severe it is an unforgettably rich and beautiful confection.

Two blocks to the east lies Mountjoy Square, of which the north and east sides are intact, the other two sides having become ruinous. However some sense of its original grandeur can be obtained by walking through the Corporation Park at its centre. A short detour into the inner suburbs will bring the traveller to a perfect and lovingly restored gem of classical architecture, the Casino at Marino, built in 1758 to the design of Sir William Chambers and now open to the public.

DAVID NORRIS
Further information on the buildings of Dublin may be had from:
Dublin City Association of An Taisce (National Trust for Ireland), Tailors' Hall, Back Lane, Dublin 8
Dublin Tourism, O'Connell Street, Dublin
Irish Georgian Society, Leixlip Castle, Leixlip, Co Kildare

STAIRCASES
The wrought iron staircase of Ely House (below and inset), with its carved panels of gilt wood showing the Labours of Hercules, is unique in Dublin. The craftsman is unknown. Left: detail from the balustrade at Belvedere House, decorated with bronze Apollo medallions

Literary Dublin

With her 'gentle veils of rain and all her ghosts that walk', Dublin has produced a disproportionate number of the world's great writers. Dean Swift, James Joyce, W B Yeats, Oscar Wilde and Sean O'Casey were all Dubliners, and the literary life goes on today with innovative work in the theatre.

JONATHAN SWIFT
Gulliver's awakening in Lilliput from Gulliver's Travels, *Swift's scathing satire on politics and society. Swift was much concerned by poverty in Ireland and campaigned vigorously for Irish freedom*

from English trade restrictions. The Drapier's Letters, *exposing a scheme to introduce poor-quality copper coinage to the country, made him a national hero. The bust is at St Patrick's Cathedral where he was Dean*

Dublin has a long and distinguished history stretching back to medieval times, when uniquely among Irish cities Dublin had its own Mystery Play. Irish people have also always been great lovers of books as objects, as the rich decoration of the *Book of Kells* as well as the beautifully tooled book bindings of the 18th century testify, and the visitor who is interested in these things should not miss a visit to such superb collections as those held by the Library of Trinity College, Marsh's Library (close to St Patrick's Cathedral) and the Chester Beatty Library in Shrewsbury Road, which has an unparalleled display of Islamic and Oriental material. The interest in books continues today and the per capita purchase of books in the Republic is among the highest in the European community. Nevertheless an appetite to possess and decorate books is only one manifestation of interest in literature and Ireland, in particular Dublin, has produced a disproportionate number of the world's great writers. Some, like Joyce and O'Casey, have so clear a connection with the city of their birth that it is impossible to think of them as anything other than Irish. With others, however, the national identification is less clear, especially since by historical accident most of our contribution has been made in the English rather than the Irish language, and although this is fortunate in that it allows access to a much wider audience, it is somewhat galling to find figures such as Swift, Wilde and Shaw so frequently described as 'English' writers. Few nowadays recall that even Richard Steele, the great essayist who, with his friend Joseph Addison, founded and edited the *Tatler* (1709) and the *Spectator* (1711), was a Dubliner.

Two periods stand out very clearly as important ages in the history of literary Dublin – the 18th century, and the early 20th century. The personality that dominates 18th-century Dublin is unquestionably that of Jonathan Swift, Dean of St Patrick's Cathedral, polemicist pamphleteer and novelist. Born in Dublin in 1667 he at first had political ambitions, but his biting tongue and gift for political satire made him too feared by the establishment for advancement, and having been made Dean of St Patrick's in 1713 he remained there for the rest of his life. He is buried near the tablet in the cathedral which bears his own Latin inscription informing the world that he

has gone *ubi saeva indignatio ulterius cor lacerare nequit* – 'where savage indignation can no longer lacerate the heart'. Savage as his indignation was, he employed it in the service of humanity and his acid pen was used equally to puncture folly and pretence and to protect the defenceless. He is remembered internationally for *Gulliver's Travels*, often thought of incorrectly as a children's book but in reality of universal appeal and application. In Dublin he is recalled also as the author of *The Drapier's Letters*, which successfully exposed and prevented the perpetration of a massive financial fraud by the government, and *A Modest Proposal*, which with bitter irony demonstrated that the children of the poor would benefit materially by being treated according to the terms of animal husbandry and fattened for the pot. With a typical mixture of black humour and humane generosity he left the bulk of his estate to found a mental hospital, St Patrick's in Dublin (still serving the community), which was unique in its time in regarding the mentally ill as patients to be comforted and treated, rather than as freaks for exhibition or exposure to teasing and ridicule, which happened in the Bethlehem (Bedlam) Hospital in London. He accompanied the benefaction with a verse in which he stated that:

> *He left what little wealth he had*
> *To found a home for fools and mad*
> *And showed by one satiric touch*
> *No nation needed it so much.*

The statue of a gentler 18th-century spirit, Oliver Goldsmith, stands in contemplation outside his old university, Trinity College. Of Goldsmith's works the stage comedy *She Stoops to Conquer* (1773), the novel *The Vicar of Wakefield* (1776) and the long narrative poem written in heroic couplet form *The Deserted Village* have survived best, bearing witness to the multiplicity of his talent. Another playwright, Richard Brinsley Sheridan, also a Trinity graduate, was born in Dublin in 1751. The house in which he was born in Dorset Street was marked with a commemorative plaque some years ago and shortly thereafter demolished. It is just as well he left behind him a monument more lasting than brass, his comedy *The Rivals* (1775) which introduced to the world the immortal Mrs Malaprop. Her resentment of 'Aspersions to my parts of speech' and statement that 'If I reprehend anything in the world it is the use of my oracular tongue and a nice derangement of epitaphs' are included in almost every dictionary of literary quotations. A third playwright of an earlier generation but again a Trinity graduate was William Congreve, one of the father figures of Restoration Drama, at least two of whose plays, *Love for Love* and *The Way of the World*, are still produced all over the world with commercial success.

ABBEY THEATRE
Yeats's foundation of the Abbey Theatre with Lady Gregory, Edward Martyn and Annie Horniman was one of the most important events of the so-called Irish literary Renaissance. Controversy surrounded its performances from the beginning when Yeats's own play *The Countess Cathleen* was condemned as heretical by members of the Roman Catholic hierarchy. Two of the other great playwrights attracted to the Abbey by Yeats's experiments, J M Synge, born in the Dublin suburb of Rathfarnham in 1871 and Sean O'Casey, born in Dorset Street in 1884, also caused a storm with their original contributions to the theatre. Synge's first play *The Shadow of the Glen* (1903) was described in the press as 'an insult to every decent woman in Ireland', while his tragedy *Riders to the Sea* (1904) was deemed 'unfit for presentation on the stage'. The climax came with his now acclaimed comedy *The Playboy of the Western World* in January 1907. Throughout the first week the play evoked riots and a large body of police had to be deployed to quell the audience and protect the author. This was one of the not inconsiderable number of occasions in the Irish theatre on which at least as much drama occurred in the audience as on the stage. Synge died tragically early of cancer in 1909, but his plays now form part of the classical repertory of Irish drama.

Sean O'Casey, self-educated and reared in the tenement slums of the north city, was almost 40 when his first play based on 'the troubles' in Ireland was accepted by the Abbey Theatre. Just as Synge had brought the melody of Irish rural speech

to the stage, so O'Casey turned his genius to recreating in the theatre the subversive wit of the Dublin poor. His second play *Juno and the Paycock* was an enormous success but the next, *The Plough and the Stars*, about the rising of Easter Week 1916 provoked an explosion similar to the *Playboy* riots, allegedly because it contained a scene in which the revolutionary flag was brought into a public house frequented by prostitutes, a class of person Dublin preferred to think it did not possess. O'Casey was bitterly disappointed when in 1928 the Abbey Board decided to reject his expressionist play about World War I, *The Silver Tassie*. He settled permanently in the south of England where he died in 1964. However, he never forgot Dublin and the atmosphere of the city at the turn of the century as well as the quality of his own generous but quirky personality comes through clearly in the six volumes of his autobiography from *I knock at the door* to *Sunset and Evening Star*.

JAMES JOYCE
Another writer who never forgot Dublin despite long absence from it was the novelist James Joyce who took the city and its inhabitants as his sole subject. Joyce was born into comfortable circumstances in suburban Dublin in 1882, but his father's bibulous incapacity for dealing with the family finances soon drove them to a life of poverty, although Joyce did somehow manage to receive an excellent education from the Jesuits at Clongowes Wood, Belvedere College and University College Dublin. Joyce was remarkably unsentimental about his native city, refusing to collaborate in its squalor by speaking of 'Dear Dirty Dublin', and labelling it the Centre of Paralysis, referring to its inhabitants as the 'most hopeless, useless and inconsistent race of characters' he had ever come across. Indeed in the

OLIVER GOLDSMITH
'Even children followed, with endearing wile . . . illustration from The Deserted Village *(above). The young Goldsmith (top) ran away from Trinity College and later lost all the money intended for law studies in London by gambling in Dublin. Kind-hearted, he pursued a chequered career before making his name as a writer, and died in debt*

ABBEY THEATRE
Controversy and riots were sparked off by early productions at the Abbey, which was founded by Yeats and friends and became the flagship of the Irish literary Renaissance. The posters (left) are from the new Abbey, built after a disastrous fire in 1951

posthumously published fragment *Stephen Hero* he described the brown brick houses of Dublin as representing 'the incarnation of paralysis'. His first two books *Dubliners* and *A Portrait of the Artist as a Young Man* analyse the pressures in Irish society that he felt caused this paralysis. Nevertheless he once told a friend that just as Mary felt that when she died the word 'Calais' would be found written on her heart, so after his death 'Dublin' would be found inscribed on his.

In his work there is a minute particularity of location, so that as he said himself, if Dublin were destroyed it could be rebuilt from the pages of *Ulysses*. This gigantic comic novel, published in Paris in 1922, is regarded as one of the great turning points in modern fiction, with its pioneering of the so-called 'stream of consciousness' technique. It is a multi-faceted recreation of one day, 16 June 1904, in the life of Dublin and its citizens – the day in fact upon which its author first walked out at Sandymount with the simple, elegant, Galway girl Nora Barnacle who was to become his lifelong companion. His last work, *Finnegan's Wake*, is so experimental in technique that doubts have been expressed as to whether it can be described as a novel at all. It is certainly a difficult text for the uninitiated to decipher, but listened to when read by a skilled actor it is a unique distillation of the essence of the city he both loved and hated. Many other prose writers, notably George Moore, Oliver Gogarty, Flann O'Brien, James Plunkett, J P Donleavy, Lee Dunne, Val Mulkerns and Maeve Binchy, have written hauntingly and humorously about Dublin, but none has given its image so definitively to the world as Joyce. The Martello Tower at Sandycove, setting of the opening scene of *Ulysses*, has been made into a James Joyce Museum in his honour.

ULSTER POETS

Of course not all those who have written about Dublin have been Dubliners themselves. The Ulster poet Louis McNeice writes movingly about Dublin:

> *With her seedy elegance*
> *With her gentle veils of rain*
> *And all her ghosts that walk*
> *And all that hide behind*
> *Her Georgian façades.*

His fellow poet from Monaghan, Patrick Kavanagh, said that the worst mistake he ever made was coming to Dublin but he nevertheless celebrated in his verse the inner suburbs of the city—Baggot Street, Pembroke Road and the Banks of the Grand Canal. One of his lyrics, *Raglan Road*, recalls a chance encounter on a suburban street, the words fitted to an old Irish air 'the Dawning of the Day'.

> *On Raglan Road on an autumn day I met*
> *her first and knew*
> *That her dark hair would weave a snare that*
> *I might one day rue.*

An institution of the Dublin literary scene to which Kavanagh was much attached was the literary pub, such as McDaid's in Harry Street, the Bailey and Davy Byrne's (which has murals by Cecil Salkeld, Brendan Behan's father-in-law) in Duke Street and the Palace Bar in Fleet Street. Many of these, however, have come to the notice of the tourist – through novels or volumes of reminiscences by writers such as Anthony Cronin or John Ryan—and the whims of the publicity-shy literati have carried them off elsewhere. However, in most Dublin pubs you are likely to find the raw material of talk upon which so many writers drew.

MOORE'S MELODIES

In 19th century Dublin, poetry predominated with figures such as Thomas Moore who staked his reputation on the enormously long *Lalla Rookh* which is now almost forgotten, although his *Irish Melodies*, poems such as *The Last Rose of Summer* and *She is far from the land*, written to fit the rhythmic pattern of traditional Irish airs, remain popular items in the concert repertoire of tenor singers. In *Ulysses* James Joyce, who disliked the sentimentality of many of the 'melodies', has his character Leopold Bloom reflect on glancing at the statue of the poet in College Green that they did right to install the image of the author of 'The Meeting of the Waters' on top of a gents' urinal. The statue is still there, but the subterranean loo is closed, its roof used as a base for rainfall-measuring instruments. A less fortunate poet was James Clarence Mangan, who died in 1849, is the author or translator of the patriotic poem *Dark* indeed even from languages he did not understand, or had invented himself. Mangan, who died in 1849, is the author or translator of the patriotic poem *Dark Rosaleen*. Addicted to opium and alcohol he had a miserable life seeking refuge from the world among the venerable tomes of the Trinity College Library where he held a lowly clerkship. Happier in life was the Northerner Sir Samuel Ferguson, one of the early cultural nationalists who for many years held a brilliant salon at his residence No 20 North Great George's

Street, a fine 18th-century mansion in the heart of the city. In the field of drama Ireland's main contribution was probably made by Dion Boucicault, born in 1820 in a house in Gardiner Street which is now demolished. Renowned for the creation of melodramas such as *The Colleen Bawn* and *Conn the Shaughraun*, with his mastery of theatrical effect he influenced not only Irish dramatists like Sean O'Casey and Brendan Behan, both born within a stone's throw of Gardiner Street themselves, but also, through his tours of the US, American playwrights like Tennessee Williams and Eugene O'Neill.

YEATS AND WILDE

The second half of the 19th century saw the birth in the Dublin suburb of Sandymount, in 1867, of one of the world's greatest poets, the Nobel prizewinner William Butler Yeats. The Yeats family were from Sligo, and Yeats, although he was educated at the High School, Dublin (then in Harcourt Street) and spent a good deal of his young manhood in London, hankered for the west of Ireland. This spirit infuses much of his melodic early poetry such as *The Lake Isle of Innisfree*, *Down by the Salley Gardens* and *The Stolen Child*. The progenitor of the Celtic Twilight and the Abbey Theatre, he was made a Senator of the newly formed Free State, serving from 1922 to 1928, and his home on the west side of Merrion Square carries a commemorative plaque.

Across the Square at No 1 lived Sir William and Lady Wilde, the parents of Oscar Wilde, who was born around the corner in Westland Row in 1856. Sir William was a distinguished eye surgeon and antiquarian, and, in marked contrast to his eldest son, a determined womaniser, a fact which does not seem to have greatly troubled his wife who concentrated on writing a great volume of nationalistic verse under the pen name of Speranza. Oscar Wilde was one of the most brilliant undergraduates in the Trinity of his day, but soon made his way to Oxford where he won the Newdigate Prize and made a reputation for the eccentricity of his dress and the scintillating wit of his conversation. His own view of the Irish was that we are 'a nation of brilliant failures, but the greatest talkers since the Greeks'. Indeed the term Wildean has become an accolade of brilliance in conversation. His first successful work was a novel, *The Picture of Dorian Gray*, a stylised *Roman-à-clef* full of symbolic references to his homosexual inclinations that were subsequently turned against him at his notorious trials in London. He was a master of epigram and of paradox, defined by Chesterton as 'truth standing on its head to attract attention' ('work is the curse of the drinking classes', says one of Wilde's characters) and he took London by storm producing four superb comedies in quick succession – *Lady Windermere's Fan* in 1892, *A Woman of No Importance* in 1893, *An Ideal Husband* and *The Importance of Being Earnest* in 1895.

THEATRE TODAY

It should not be felt that Dublin's literary life is all in the past. In the fifties and sixties there was a significant revival in the theatre with the presentation of original works by a new generation of Irish playwrights – Samuel Beckett, Brendan Behan and Hugh Leonard – and an international theatre festival of some distinction was established. This takes place annually in October and up to 50 plays from all over the world are performed in a three-week period. The Theatre Festival has an office in Nassau Street. Of the theatres themselves, the Abbey Theatre, rebuilt on its original site in Abbey Sreet after a disastrous fire in 1951, has become a national institution, while the Gaiety Theatre in North King Street, at the top of Grafton Street, and the Olympia Theatre in Dame Sreet have been recently refurbished. One delightful smaller theatre is the Gate Theatre in the Rotunda Complex at the top of O'Connell Street. The Gate developed an international reputation under the guidance of its reigning partnership of Micheal MacLiammoir and Hilton Edwards for nearly 40 years from the early 1930s, training actors like Orson Welles who went on to international stardom. After they had both died in the 1970s fears were expressed for its survival, but in recent years a new eminently successful and innovative management under the direction of Michael Colgan has made it one of the most exciting and popular theatrical venues in the city. Also of interest is the Project Theatre and Art Gallery in East Essex Street, where interesting experimental work has been carried out by the playwright Peter Sheridan and his director/producer brother Jim Sheridan. A smaller but vital theatre is the Focus Theatre just behind Leeson Street, where Deirdre O'Connell has brought her experience of the Stanislavsky Studio in New York to bear on the plays of Ibsen and Strindberg, among others. There are also a number of vigorous peripatetic theatrical companies such as Rough Magic, Smock Alley, and the enterprising and talented Horizon Theatre Co who delight the Dublin public with their annual free Shakespeare performances in summertime in St Stephen's Green.

Wherever you walk in Dublin you can be sure that you are close to some aspect of literary history and there is always the chance that in some dark corner of a Dublin pub, talking to a shabbily dressed Dubliner, you may yourself, like many of the unsuspecting Dubliners of an earlier vintage, be providing copy for an aspiring O'Casey or Joyce.

DAVID NORRIS
Elected to the Irish Senate in 1987, David Norris is a lecturer in English at Trinity College, and is closely involved with the North Great George's Street Preservation Society and James Joyce Foundation of Ireland.

POET AND WIT
Portrait of W B Yeats by his brother Jack, at the National Gallery (top). Yeats, along with George Bernard Shaw, was among those who sought to defend the reputation of Oscar Wilde (Vanity Fair caricature, above) when the scandal broke of Wilde's affair with the Marquess of Queensberry's son

Traditional Music

FIDDLERS
At the Cultúrlann in Monkstown, on Dublin Bay. The fiddle's range and expressiveness makes it ideal for dance music and more reflective tunes

I ntricate variations on an age-old tune, 'battering' out the steps of a country dance, sing-along sessions at the pub, feasts of music for musicians from round the world . . . all these are aspects of traditional Irish music, which began in farmhouse kitchens and now enjoys new life as an essential part of the city scene.

One of the most attractive features of Dublin night life – for visitor and native alike – is the number of music and singing pubs which flourish both in the city centre and suburbs. The music provided in these establishments varies from sing-along with piano accompaniment to organised groups in ballad sessions or informal sessions of instrumental traditional music to which the listeners may from time to time dance Irish country-dances or 'sets'.

Traditional (or folk) music has an unusually high profile in Ireland. There are several reasons for this. It did not suffer the same eclipse in Ireland as it did with the Industrial Revolution in many countries, and in consequence it was still popular in the early decades of the 20th century. After World War II, when the emerging international pop culture threatened traditional music, a group of Irish musicians got together to promote it.

CÉILÍ NIGHTS
At the turn of the century, Irish traditional music was the popular music favoured by the vast majority of the Irish people. In the countryside and in the numerous small towns and villages, it was the music played when people assembled in someone's home, at crossroads or in village halls, for a 'night', 'scoraíocht', or 'soirée'. The most basic and frequent of these events was the session at the céilí-house — or scoraíochting-house – there being some such house in every townland. It might be any house in the area that was suitably situated, and where the good man and woman of the house liked music and company and didn't make too much fuss about getting to bed at an early hour. Preferably it would have a spacious kitchen with a stone-flagged floor.

At these houses the young men and girls, as well as some of the older folk from a radius of half a mile or so, would assemble on a couple of nights a week. There might be as many as twenty-five or thirty people involved, or as few as seven or eight. They whiled away the hours between milking time and bedtime – both conveniently variable – with talking, card-playing, story-telling or dancing.

Sets or half-sets would be the order of the night – traditional group dances, usually danced by four couples. There are numerous regional kinds and variations. In some parts of the country, however, the Lancers, the barn-dance and even the waltz were not unknown. The music would be provided on a fiddle or concertina, or if need be one of the company would lilt the required tunes.

Dancers who prided themselves on their footwork vied with one another in 'battering' out intricate rhythms on the stout flags of the farmhouse kitchen floor. (Battering in this context refers to the dancers' lively footwork.) There might be a few songs, usually comic songs or songs about some local incident. In areas where there was a strong singing tradition, there might be a particular house or night for singing rather than dancing, but music and dancing were the rule.

These nights of music-making took place all the year round, though in many areas they were either abandoned or operated at a low key during Lent. There were also 'special nights', such as balls, weddings and threshing nights. These were attended by large numbers of people so that not only the house but also the barn or some such spacious outhouse would be used. It was common practice throughout most of the country that all musicians who were willing to play had an open invitation to such functions. So it was that the musician was frequently to be seen heading homewards to the song of the lark in the morning.

Travelling musicians who sang and played at markets and fairs helped to bring tunes and songs from one area to another. Travelling and local musicians were also willing, for a few pence per lesson – or sometimes, in the case of the former, for their keep – to pass on their skills and tunes to aspiring youngsters.

Such then, was the standing and place of Irish traditional music in the lives of the people in the greater part of rural Ireland about the turn of the century. The cities, such as Dublin, Cork, Galway and Belfast, also had traditional music communities where immigrants from the provinces compared and swapped tunes with the native traditional musicians.

DECLINE AND REVIVAL
The 1930s and 1940s were poor times in Ireland, and emigration seemed set to drain perpetually the life blood of youth from her shores. At this time Irish music was flourishing and popular amongst the Irish emigrants in the cities of England and the USA. Michael Coleman, the most celebrated of all Irish traditional fiddlers, recorded more than 60 records in New York in the 1920s and 1930s. But at home, the Dance Halls Act was opening the way for commercial dance halls where modern dance bands were introducing the foxtrot, the tango and the hokey cokey in an

INSTRUMENTS
Of the instruments normally used in playing Irish traditional music the only uniquely Irish instrument is the uilleann pipes, so called because these sweet-sounding pipes are blown by a bellows under the arm and elbow (uilleann is the Gaelic for elbow). The fiddle, the two-row accordion, the wooden concert flute and the tin whistle will be found to the fore in any big session, and the banjo too is very popular. The concertina, piano accordion and mandolin are less widely played, except for Co Clare where the concertina has for many years been very much in favour, especially with lady musicians. The harp, for long the national emblem, was once Ireland's foremost musical instrument, and has seen a revival in recent years. The guitar, the bouzouki and the piano are the instruments mostly used for accompaniment, though O Riada, and later the Bothy Band favoured the harpsichord. The bodhran, a simple hand-held goatskin drum, is widely used, and one may also find the rhythms being tapped out with a pair of bones or spoons. Drums are usually used in céilí bands

atmosphere far removed from the house-dance scene. Young people were flocking in thousands to these 'Ballrooms of Romance' and, for a period at least, the era of the céilí-house-dance was at an end. The morale among musicians was at a low ebb and attitudes to the music were unenlightened, even derisory.

Since music in the pubs had not been the practice up to this time, there were very few places where the traditional musician could find an appreciative audience. Many were inclined to put away the fiddles and the flutes entirely, but a determined core of musicians, who met regularly at the Pipers' Club at 14 Thomas Street in the Dublin Liberties, decided that they would organise an annual nationwide gathering of musicians. Having made contact with fellow enthusiasts in other parts of the country, they planned the first Fleadh Cheoil (literally a 'feast of music') which took place in Mullingar in May 1951. It was successful enough to warrant another try, and so was born the traditional music organisation Comhaltas Ceoltóirí Éireann (literally Fellowship of Musicians of Ireland) and the Fleadhanna Cheoil.

FIRST FLEADHANNA
Those first Fleadhanna Cheoil (literally 'feasts of music') gave traditional musicians a platform where they could play to a really appreciative audience and where traditional style was the rule. The sun always seemed to shine at those early Fleadhanna too, as men and women took down fiddles and flutes that had lain idle for years and hit the road for Cavan and Loughrea with lightness in their step and a tune in their hearts.

While the primary purpose of the Fleadhanna Cheoil was (and continues to be) the holding of competitions on various instruments, many musicians came just for the sheer enjoyment of playing music and meeting musicians arriving from other

areas. Informal sessions of music, in pubs and on the streets, would go on all day and into the early hours, and although the Fleadh officially concluded on Monday evening, the music and revelry would last well into mid-week. Within the space of a few years the mood of the Irish music would have swung from depression to an all time 'high'.

Through the 1950s the Fleadh and Comhaltas grew hand in hand. Irish exiles soon began to take an active part and musicians living in Liverpool, Birmingham, London and New York began coming over to the Fleadh, and so another dimension was added. Branches of Comhaltas sprang up all over Ireland, organising classes, concerts and sessions at local level. With a countrywide network of activity established from the mid-1950s or so, traditional music was already riding high by the time of the international ballad boom in the early 1960s.

The situation was further consolidated through a massive teaching campaign which commenced in the mid-1960s and through which numerous fiddlers, flute players, pipers and other musicians were encouraged to pass on their music and music styles to the younger generation. The results of this network of classes can be seen in the huge numbers of younger people – from teens to early 30s – now playing the old music in the old style.

NEW APPROACHES
With the popularisation of traditional music in an era of rapidly advancing technology and changing lifestyles, it was only to be expected that there should be new ideas and approaches, geared towards favourably presenting the music on television, on radio, and in concert hall or cabaret productions. For many years the typical group had been the céilí band, in which eight or nine musicians played in unison (mostly for dancers), with backing on piano and drums. The first major departure from this method of presentation came in the early 1960s with the formation of the group Ceoltóirí Chualann under the direction of Seán Ó Riada. This group introduced a new style of arrangement and presentation and paved the way for such diverse and exciting groups as the Chieftains, the Bothy Band and De Danann, and also for groups such as Planxty, Clanad and Stockton's Wing, who, while not confining themselves to traditional material, continued to use it extensively.

DANCING IN THE PUB
While the playing of traditional music has been common in clubs, branches of Comhaltas and music pubs from the early 1960s, it was only half a dozen years or so ago that the dancing of country sets in such places came into practice. There were areas, such as West Clare and Slieve Luachra (on the Cork/Kerry border) where 'sets in the local' had been the practice for twenty years or more. Enthusiasts who visited these areas

became eager set-dancers, and another wave of 'revival' spread throughout the country. Soon set-dancers were flocking to the traditional sessions in large numbers and in pubs or clubs where a flagged or wooden floor was underfoot and where the landlord did not object, it soon became the practice for members of the audience to 'take the floor' in response to the rhythm of lively reels or polkas.

THE PLAYER'S ART

Irish traditional music comes in two forms – vocal and instrumental. The latter is mostly dance music – reels, jigs, hornpipes, polkas, set-dances, mazurkas – the remainder being marches, slow airs (usually song tunes) and 'planxties' (harpers' pieces which have survived from the 17th or 18th centuries). These tunes have various origins, but it is possible to state generally that they were mostly composed in the 18th and 19th centuries, that they were passed down aurally through generations of music makers and that practitioners of the art of traditional music share a common approach and set of techniques in their interpretation of this music. Within this common approach there are standards – accepted by performers and enlightened listeners – by which one judges a musician's ability to interpret, rework and refurbish the old tunes, through the use of various forms of ornamentation and of melodic and rhythmic variation. These variations and ornamentations are generally minor ones, involving just a few notes in a particular phase of a tune, yet when executed with skill and subtlety they can show a considerable level of imagination and even creativity. One is more likely to find this kind of music where music is played for listening, rather than where the dance tunes are 'belted out' for a set, but even in the latter case the musician will usually try to give the tunes that little bit extra in rhythm (called 'lift' or 'swing' in traditional music) which will add extra zest to the dancing.

OLD SONGS, NEW STYLES

Traditional songs in Ireland include the old songs in Irish which may be heard in the Gaeltacht (Irish-speaking) areas along the western coast, and which are sung in what is called the 'sean nós' or 'old style'; and songs in the English language (but with an Irish character or flavour) of which there are numerous examples in various regional and personal styles.

Solo unaccompanied singing is the usual means of presentation and many traditional songs may run to eight or ten minutes, which tends to limit the appeal of traditional singing to a small circle of devotees. The best songs and singing styles demand a high degree of vocal artistry and interpretation and several of the finest traditional singers – such as Paddy Tunney and the late Seosamh Ó hÉanai – have won international recognition. But these serious demanding songs with their intricate melodies and

niceties of embellishment are not the ideal stuff for the noisy atmosphere of a pub session. A lighter, more boisterous type of song with a bit of backing is more appropriate to such a situation. With the great international 'ballad boom' of the 1960s, groups singing the lighter or simpler ballads, to guitar accompaniment, found a ready market in clubs and pubs throughout Ireland. The McPeakes of Belfast, and the Clancy Brothers and Tommy Makem were first in the field; and the Dubliners and the Wolfe Tones have been among the most successful of these groups. The old styles of solo singing still flourish, however, and may be heard at special traditional singing sessions such as the Fleadh in Ballycastle, Co Antrim, at An t-Oireachtas (the great annual Irish language festival), at the Cultúrlann, Monkstown, Co Dublin or at Fleadh Cheoil na hÉireann.

Traditional singers such as Len Graham, Kevin Cuniffe and Dolores Keane also help to introduce the old songs and styles to a wider audience, by singing the occasional solo song in traditional style, during a performance with a group.

WHERE TO HEAR IT

Traditional music, singing and dancing can be found at pubs and other venues in Dublin all year round. A list of these is given in the Directory, page 104.

Sessions are held at the Cultúrlann, 32 Belgrave Square, Monkstown, Co Dublin (easily reached by DART trains from the city centre) on Fridays and Saturdays all year round, and from Monday to Saturday from June to early September. This is the headquarters of Comhaltas Ceoltóirí Éireann.

Out of the city, the best areas for music in the pubs are Clare, Galway and South Sligo, but sessions will be found in most other areas too. Details are generally given in local papers.

Fleadhanna Cheoil are held at County and Provincial level throughout the country from May to August, culminating in the 'All Ireland' Fleadh Cheoil na hÉireann, in a different place each year.

SÉAMUS MacMATHUNA
Séamus MacMathuna is musical adviser to Comhaltas Ceoltóirí Éireann.

•●•
CONCERTINA
The 'squeezebox' was popular for old-style farmhouse music sessions. Today it is particularly favoured in Co Clare
•●•

•●•
NEW STYLE
Moving Hearts play traditional music with the help of non-traditional technology one of the strengths of the old music is its adaptability
•●•

City Crafts

WOODCARVER
One of the craftworkers at the Tower Design Craft Centre, a former sugar refinery, distillery and iron foundry refurbished as part of a scheme to revive the inner city. Visitors can see craftworkers practise their skills, and buy direct or from the shop

Dublin's barrel makers are said to have learnt their trade from St Patrick's own brewer, and it is certain that at least one Dublin firm has been practising the same craft skills for 500 years. Craftsmanship is a long and honourable tradition in the city, and today a new generation ensures that it continues to thrive.

The old 'Dublin Jack of All Trades' had a song and a street ballad all to himself. The ballad told the story of all the trades and crafts and the special streets of Dublin, each with its own type of workers.

> *In Sackville Street he was a Pastry Cook,*
> *In James Street a Baker,*
> *In Cook Street he did coffins make,*
> *In Eustace Street a Preacher.*

The ballad was written by an author who knew his Dublin streets like the back of his hand. The pastrycooks started their trade in the street of the cooks up at the back of Adam and Eve's Church. This street was built outside the old walls of Dublin in case the pastrycooks set fire to the city. They had their own trade guild under the special patronage of St James the Apostle, who, we are told by tradition, used to boil the billy can and make the Irish stew for his Master and the other eleven apostles. According to the poem of 1767, in the *Calendar of Ancient Records of Dublin* (edited by Lady Gilbert in 1904), the pastrycooks held the 10th position in the annual muster of the 25 trade guild corporations, who 'rode the fringes' and the Liberties of Dublin on coal-black horses. The 18th-century bard who pictured them going by spoke of their banners and their colours:

> *Orange and black, silks, satins*
> *Feathers and plumes.*
> *Next march the Cooks who study day and night,*
> *With costly fare to please the appetite.*
> *With these the Vintners ride, did they refine*
> *As much as they adulterate the wine,*
> *Their every muse would gladly sound*
> *And with what pleasure would the glass go round.*

The pastrycooks are still in Sackville Street, now called O'Connell Street, and all over Dublin City and suburbs you will find pastrycooks' windows with a display of delights to dazzle the eyes and whet the appetite. St James the Apostle has truly smiled on the cooks of Dublin.

COOPERS, TAILORS AND SCRIBES

If the disappearance of vintners who mix water with the wine is not to be lamented,

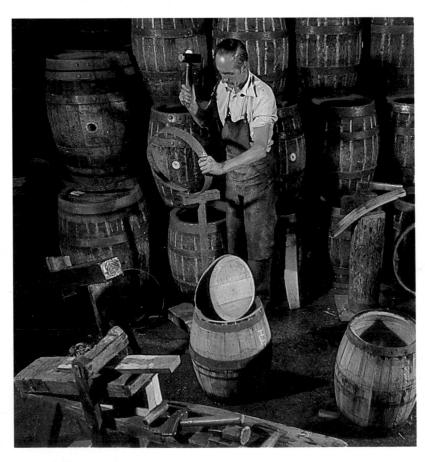

COOPER
Shaping, softening and bending the staves to make a barrel is a long process but it will be watertight for years if damaged staves are properly replaced. Nowadays Dublin's coopers find more demand for plantholders than beer casks like this, but the same skills are needed

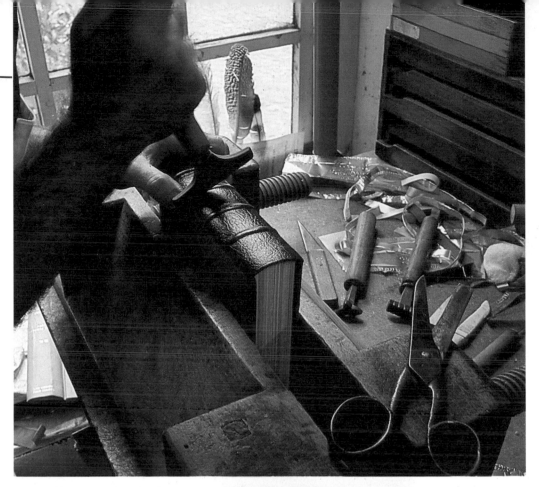

the decline of another craft related to drink certainly is. The use of motor tankers for porter (or stout) put the popular Liffey barges, Guinness's sailors and the barrel-making coopers of Abbey Street out of business – the coopers' 'wake' was held in the Clarence Hotel on Wellington Quay. This is a lovely trade, a craft said to have been introduced by St Patrick's brewer, Mescan, who showed the Dublin men how to make casks and barrels in the 5th century. In the rhyme, the coopers were in the 17th position in the line-up of the guilds when they rode the fringes, wearing green and white and carrying a banner of their patron, St Patrick, casting out the snakes. The coopers were also in James Street and the Liberties, and over on the north bank in Smithfield. Their first guild hall was in Castle Street and they later moved into the Tailors' Hall in Back Lane. There are still some coopers in Dublin: a handful are keeping the craft alive by turning out beautiful buckets, flower pots, shrub boxes, umbrella stands and fireside turf or log barrels.

The cross-legged Tailors next in order go
Who by their arts trim others for this show.
No wonder then, those Tailors march so gay
Since from all others thus they bear the sway.

The merchant tailors, under the banner of St John the Baptist, in their Saxon blue and white suits, took second place in the rhyme behind the Merchants' Guild of the Most Holy Trinity. Now there are perhaps a dozen master tailors who ply their skills each day in the city, making hand-made suits and finery. The place to see such finery is Capel Street, which has more men's clothing shops than any other street in Dublin. James Joyce said it was the best street in the city and Joyce was a stylish

dresser, with cricket shirts and blazers all hand-made. The early 18th-century Tailors' Hall is the only remaining old guildhall in Dublin. It is well worth a look, across the street from Christ Church.

James Joyce is better known for his part in Dublin's great literary tradition – this is the city of scribes, illuminators, and storytellers, the writers and the makers of books. From the earliest Irish Church Mass Book of St Maelruin, written in Tallaght, Co Dublin, the city has had generations of writers. Dean Swift, Brinsley Sheridan, Thomas Moore, Wolf Tone, Robert Emmet, James Clarence Mangan, Oscar Wilde, Sean O'Casey, James Joyce, J M Synge, Shaw, Austin Clarke and Brendan Behan all have one thing in common: they are all 'Dubs', all born in Dublin.

But Dublin is also the place to admire

BOOKBINDER
A Dublin speciality seen at Marlay Park, Rathfarnham, where a 200-year old courtyard has been converted into craft workshops

SILK PAINTER
Exclusive, hand-painted silk at the Tower Design Craft Centre—both new and old craft skills are practised in Dublin

the physical manufacture of books. Trinity College is the home of the *Book of Kells*, the *Book of Durrow* and the *Book of Armagh*, and at Marsh's Library the fine craft of bookbinding can be admired, a craft that survives in the city today.

SOAP AND CANDLES

At the top of Westland Row, birthplace of Oscar Wilde and site of the chapel where Leopold Bloom saw the holy water at low tide in the water font, they still sell the lemon soap which Leopold Bloom bought, in Sweny's Chemist Shop.

Soap-makers were led by St George and the Dragon, in the trade guilds procession – they were among the Masters, Wardens and Brotherhood Fraternity of the ancient Tallow Chandlers, Soap Boilers and Wax Light Makers, which brings us to one of Dublin's most venerable crafts. What other city has one firm with a tradition of 500 years of manufacturing candles? Since at least 1488, for five centuries, Rathbornes have been making candles. It is a fine sight to see Robert Leppla hand-casting a beeswax church candle, not only as his father did, but as the Dublin candle-makers have done for 500 years. The Rathborne family came from Chester in England and started their wax chandlers' workshops in Wyne Tavern Street. Close by is the Church of St Werburgh, dating back to the 12th century, and it is possible that the first Rathbornes came to Dublin at this period: Chester Cathedral was originally St Werburgh's Abbey. It is said that the Rathbornes made candles which could be bought by the poor, who would have used rush-lights before. Rathbornes are now in East Wall Road.

When the parade was over, when the fringes were ridden and when the Liberties boundaries were marked, the trade guilds adjourned for refreshments. The Tallow Chandlers' Guild paid for a fine dinner and a few glasses of ale for St George, but the poor dragon had to fend for himself: the chief clerk of the guildhall in Keyzars Lane, Jonathan Callbeck, recorded in the minutes that the dragon had to provide his own dinner. In a later age, Sunlight Chambers at the corner of Parliament Street and Essex Quay was the charming construction of Lever Brothers and Barringtons Soap Manufacturers. Barringtons had been making soap in Dublin since 1775. As a child in Dublin

CANDLE MAKER
Rathbornes have been making candles for over 500 years. Here the wicks are dipped and re-dipped in beeswax or (above) have it poured over them, to make fine church candles. Thousands of paraffin wax candles are also made by machine each year, for household use

city I washed myself every day in William Lever's wonderful yellow Sunlight Soap. Red carbolic was for the clothes and the wooden scrubbing board, and Monkey Brand dirt shifter was for the lino floors and to bring back the natural grain of the floor timber. Sunlight Chambers is still a beautiful building. The figures sculpted on the building represent one interpretation of the toil of mankind and womankind: men working and dirtying their clothes and the women washing the clothes with soap.

STEPPING BACK IN TIME

From Sunlight Chambers, walk along Parliament Street towards City Hall to find the oldest cutlers in Europe, dating back to the year 1670. To step through the door of Thomas Read's shop at 4 Parliament Street is to step back through time. Some of the display cases come from an older premises in Crane Lane, where Read's still have a workshop. Sword cases can be seen here, from the days when Read's made swords; they also made instruments for the surgeons at the Royal College of Surgeons in St Stephen's Green. Cutlers paraded with Painters, Stainers and Stationers under the banner and protection of St Luke, the Evangelist.

On the way down to Read's look out for a craftsman tailor, an antique book shop and Mason's, making scientific instruments. Across the street at No 12 was the headquarters of the Fenians, which was situated right under the nose of Dublin Castle. This was where they published the *Irish People* newspaper. Many of the Fenians were in the building trade, and their brick, stone and plasterwork can be seen in the city's fine Victorian buildings and churches. The father of a Mason's employee made the key which was smuggled into Richmond Prison to help James Stephens, the Fenian Chief, escape in 1865. Further along the street, Garnetts and Keegans are famous for fishing tackle and hand fly tying, perhaps for the salmon of knowledge that swims up the Liffey every day.

PROUD WEAVERS

The Weavers next in order proudly ride,
Who with great skill the nimble shuttle guide,
Pity such art should meet such small reward
But what art nowadays does meet regard?
Out of the city centre is Damien Shine,

who welcomes visitors to his cloth fulling and napping mills in Rowerston Lane, Old Kilmainham, where monks had fulling mills in the 8th century. The mills are on the land of St Maignead, which became the property of the Knights Hospitallers of St John of Jerusalem, and they too had mills. The Crock of Gold Weavers and Dyers always give a 'Cead Mile Failte' – a thousand welcomes – at Newtownpark Avenue, Blackrock, Co Dublin. The last of the old Liberty weavers was the late Padraig Breathnach, now thought by his friends to be surely weaving banners for the Huguenots beyond the pearly gates.

CRAFTS TODAY

Goldsmiths, silversmiths, gunsmiths, blacksmiths, whitesmiths (who worked with tin) and more have nearly all been supplanted by new techniques and only a handful are left. And yet today new crafts and skills are constantly being created and old crafts revived by the young people of Dublin and elsewhere in Ireland. In the Liberties you could find a coppersmith using Viking techniques; in Pearse Street you might find workers in gold, silver and pewter – and hand-makers of chocolates. Every year the Irish Goods Council Craft Fair is held in the Royal Dublin Societies Exhibition Hall in Ballsbridge and each year it gets bigger and better. Specialities that were never heard of in the days of the old trade guilds can be seen, from flowers to jewels and glass, from leather to pottery, from lace to wool, from toys to boats. The best places to see people at work (and buy craft items) are the Marlay Park craft centre in Rathfarnham, under the wide range of Dublin mountains, and in the city at IDA Enterprises in the Tower Design Craft Centre, Pearse Street. The skills of the workshops may change, but in recent years have ranged from harp-making, heraldry and stained glass to dolls and knitwear, as well as jewellery and pottery. In spite of mass-production and the modern taste for standardisation, Dublin remains a city of craftworkers, developing new skills and ensuring that the old ones continue to thrive.

ÉAMONN MAC THOMÁIS
A bard of Dublin for the 20th century, Éamonn Mac Thomáis has written several books and made over 20 films on the city, where he has always lived.

THE USE OF SOAP

Sculptured frieze on the wall of Sunlight Chambers, Parliament Street. This was the headquarters in Dublin of Lever Brothers: red carbolic was for the clothes, Monkey Brand for the floors but 'wonderful yellow Sunlight Soap' was best of all

Gardens
of
Dublin County

T hink of Ireland and you think of lush green gardens and parks and a landscape of true natural beauty. The gentle climate which makes Ireland so green favours horticulture, and in Dublin's gardens can be seen many tender and exotic plants.

William Butler Yeats wrote of those 'gardens where a soul's at ease', and within short distances of the centre of this busy city weary travellers will find such tranquil gardens, flower-filled and enhanced with emerald green lawns. Each has its own character, its own setting, and above all its own charm.

What makes an Irish garden special? The mild, moist climate is a major contributing factor. Mildness is a relative matter, but Ireland does not suffer from the excesses of frost and snow, or sun and drought, that can hamper gardeners in some other lands. Ireland's gardeners do complain too often about the rain, but that very rain helps to keep their lawns green through the summer, and provides the moisture to enable the cultivation of some most exotic plants. But the more ordinary plants flourish too, and the visitor can discover the very finest spring bulbs and roses, many of them raised here by world-famous breeders.

The Dublin area is not the mildest part of Ireland, but the coastal fringe enjoys an enviable climate for gardening. Frost is infrequent within sight of the sea, and as long as there is shelter from the east winds of winter, exotic plants from all over the world will flourish. So within the region about Dublin it is possible to see some of those rare plants for which Irish gardens are famous – tree-ferns from Tasmania, rhododendrons from western China, and the blue crocus from Chile.

Landscape and soil also have significant effects upon gardens. About Dublin, especially to the south, an acid soil prevails and this enables gardeners to cultivate camellias and rhododendrons with consummate ease. But the heavy clays of the counties lying west of the city are not barren; these places do have harsher winters, but fine aboreta – at Birr Castle, for example – with incomparable collections of rare trees have been established there, and should not be overlooked by keen gardeners.

FORMAL GARDENS
Undoubtedly the finest use of the landscape is seen at Powerscourt, where a superb formal garden, rising terrace by terrace from a small lake, is overshadowed by the Dublin Mountains. The Sugarloaf

THOMAS MOORE ROSE
In the Botanic Gardens—a descendant of the poet's 'Last Rose of Summer'

PHOENIX PARK
Minutes away from the heart of the city are 1752 acres of trees, water, deerpark—and a zoo dating from 1831

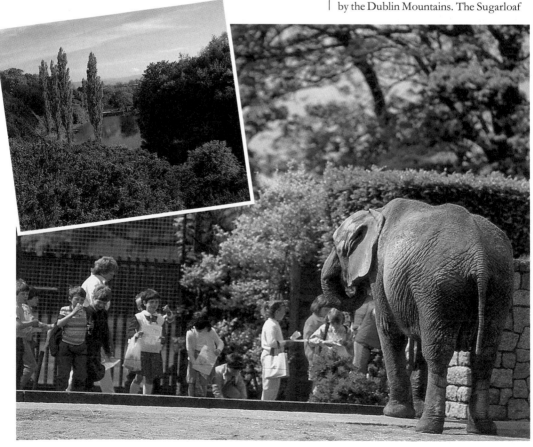

dominates the skyline, and is an integral part of the whole grand design. Nineteenth-century Powerscourt is one of the best examples of formal gardening in Ireland. Close by is Kilruddery, which predates Powerscourt by a century and more. The Sugarloaf is still visible in Kilruddery but it does not form a focal point. Instead, two parallel canals, in the French manner, lead from the house into a ride; beside them are The Angles, formal hedges of hornbeam and beech.

On an altogether grander scale is Phoenix Park; with an area of 1752 acres, it is the largest enclosed park in any European city. Its magnificent central avenue—sadly now a busy thoroughfare—is lined with beautiful trees. On crisp winter mornings when the sun shines weakly, or on warm summer afternoons, 'the Park' is a quiet haven. A herd of deer roams freely, and nestling in one sequestered corner is the Zoological Gardens, surely the prettiest zoo in Europe.

Formality prevails in the city's smaller parks. At St Anne's in Clontarf, summer beds of beautiful roses delight the eye and the nose. St Stephen's Green, in the heart of the city, and Merrion Square deserve the visitor's attention, and so does the lawned oasis of Trinity College, wherein gardens have been carefully tended for four centuries; the newest of the College squares was laid out under the supervision of Lanning Roper.

One of the least known gardens within the city limits is the Islandbridge National War Memorial, a *tour de force* of stone and formal planting which is one of the achievements of Sir Edwin Lutyens, the great English architect. Sadly neglected for many years, it is now being restored. Lutyens also restyled 14th-century Howth Castle on Dublin Bay, noted for its wild rhododendron garden begun little more than a century ago.

WILD GARDENS

The Irish character does not easily slip into imposed order, and since the mid-1800s, Irish gardeners have shyed away from rigid lines. Indeed the principles of the wild garden, in which plants have free rein to grow and multiply, were promoted by an Irishman, William Robinson. His ideas can best be appreciated in the celebrated Mount Usher Garden to the south of Dublin in Co Wicklow where a bubbling river is wrapped in a cloak of tall gum-trees. There is a stunning Mexican pine, colourful rhododendrons and a host of other exotic plants, too tender to survive out-of-doors except in the balmy, moist atmosphere of this sheltered valley. Here the plants grow naturally, the lawns are trimmed only when the flowering bulbs have set their seeds, and weedkillers are never used. And this is where that blue crocus blooms.

There is much to delight the visitor in the smaller Dublin gardens. Fernhill and the Talbot Gardens at Malahide contain collections of rare trees and shrubs,

ranging from the magnolias of the Himalayas to flame-trees of Chile, from the white-blossomed tree poppy of California to the daisy-bushes of New Zealand. Spring bulbs and the russet leaves of autumn make these, and other gardens, places for all seasons.

Of the two botanical gardens, the smaller one, only two decades old but with roots going back three hundred years and more, is maintained by Trinity College, Dublin. Both native and exotic plants are grown principally for teaching purposes, and the botanists of the University recently mounted a rescue mission to save some of the endangered plants of Mauritius – once the dodo's home.

Only two centuries have elapsed since the National Botanic Gardens was founded at Glasnevin, a short journey from central Dublin, but it is Ireland's premier garden and one of the world's greatest botanical gardens. Within there is an ancient yew walk probably planted in the 1740s, and the magnificent cast-iron glasshouse erected and designed by Richard Turner in the mid-1800s, sister to the Great Palm House of Kew Gardens in London. Tens of thousands of different plants – orchids, palms, giant water lilies, dove trees, and the native Killarney fern – are displayed in these 50 magnificent acres.

Whether the garden is large or small, formal or wild, linger a while and seek the quietude that comes with shady trees, green grass and scented flowers. About Dublin you can, with ease, find W B Yeats's 'bee-loud glade' not far from the city in beautiful Irish gardens.

DR E C NELSON
Dr E C Nelson is a Taxonomist at the National Botanic Gardens, Glasnevin.

• • •

NATIONAL BOTANIC GARDENS
Established in 1795 the gardens have thousands of species and one of the world's oldest curved glass conservatories. Before 1795 this was the poet Tickell's estate, visited by literary figures, and it remains a pleasant place to wander

• • •

CITY CENTRE

*In the Liberties—this was the name given to the area outside
the medieval city's jurisdiction, and it still has a character of
its own. For some, this is the 'real' Dublin*

ABBEY PRESBYTERIAN CHURCH

Parnell Square
A prominent landmark with its white neo-Gothic clocktower and slender spire, the church has many fine stone carvings, over the doorway and at the bases of window arches. It was completed in 1864 and the building cost of £20,000 was met by Alex Findlater, a Scot who established a leading grocery chain and brewery in Dublin; it is widely known as Findlater's Church. The church overlooks the Garden of Remembrance which commemorates those who gave their lives for Irish freedom. The Children of Lir sculpture at the west end, by Oisin Kelly, recalls a legend of children being turned into swans.

Children of Lir sculpture (see Abbey Presbyterian Church), illustrating one of Ireland's loveliest legends

ABBEY THEATRE

Marlborough Street
This stark modern block, designed by Michael Scott, replaces a smaller Abbey which opened in 1904 in a building which had been a music hall and a morgue, and which was bought and equipped as a theatre by Annie Horniman. W B Yeats, Edward Martyn and Augusta Lady Gregory were the young Abbey's moving spirits and John Millington Synge its first controversial playwright. His

Playboy of the Western World caused rioting in the theatre in 1907 among a sensitively nationalistic audience who were not prepared for its realism.

There was further rioting in the Abbey in 1926 when Sean O'Casey's *The Plough and the Stars* was first staged here. Many of the audience regarded it as a cynical view of the 1916 Rebellion. The Abbey Players achieved an international reputation but in the 1940s, with Yeats dead, it was felt that the Abbey had lost the motivation necessary to its status as a national theatre. However, a plan put forward to demolish it and build a three-part national theatre on the site was shelved after a change of Government. On 17 July 1951 the Abbey was destroyed by fire. The present Abbey and Peacock complex opened exactly 15 years later.

ALDBOROUGH HOUSE

Portland Row
A brick mansion with a granite façade, this was the last great town house of the 18th century, and was completed in 1796 for Edward Stratford, Earl of Aldborough, by William Chambers. Some of its original ornamentation in Portland stone was badly corroded by the salty air of the Bay, which then lay much closer to the house than now. In 1813 it became the Feinaglin Institute, a school using a revolutionary system of memory training. Later a barrack, and now accommodating Post Office staff, the house retains its fine interior. It overlooks the Five Lamps, a monument to Galway-born General Henry Hall of the Indian army. It is not open.

BANK OF IRELAND

College Green
Formerly the Irish Parliament House, this striking windowless edifice has 22 pillars in its grand portico, which is 147ft long. Over its pediment are figures of Hibernia, Commerce and Fidelity, and those of Fortitude, Justice and Liberty can be seen over another portico in Westmoreland Street. The main architect was Edward Lovett Pearce, and the building took from 1729 to 1739 to erect. There were later additions by James Gandon and Francis Johnston.

The former House of Commons is now the bank's cash office and

Bank of Ireland from Trinity College

may be seen during banking hours. The old House of Lords may be visited by small groups by arrangement. Its two large tapestries, depicting the Battle of the Boyne and the Siege of Derry, are well preserved. They were hung in 1735. In a recess is the mace of the old Commons Speaker. Another room in the bank has an exquisite Venus ceiling attributed to the Francini Brothers. A large dome over what is now the cash office was destroyed by fire in 1792.

The Act of Union of 1800 ended the building's days as a parliament house. Its most famous parliamentarian had been Henry Grattan, whose statue by John Henry Foley is in the roadway opposite. The nearby Thomas Davis statue is by Edward Delaney.

BELVEDERE HOUSE

Great Denmark Street
Begun in 1775 for George Rochford, Lord Belvedere, this mansion contains some of the finest plasterwork of the celebrated Michael Stapleton, including the Apollo, Diana and Venus rooms, though the Venus ceiling's centrepiece was removed when the building became a boys' college in 1841. There are fireplaces by Bossi, the Venetian master, and bronze Apollo medallions on the staircase handrails.

George Rochford died in 1814 and the house, commanding one of the finest urban views of the day down the Georgian North Great George's Street, was sold to the Jesuits 27 years later for use as a college. It is a famous rugby school, and its most celebrated pupil was undoubtedly James Joyce, who lived nearby. (He was born south of the city at 41 Brighton Square, Rathgar.)

Belvedere House is renowned for Michael Stapleton's plasterwork

Bewley's in Grafton Street: old style charm and a fragrance of coffee

BEWLEY'S CAFÉS

Grafton Street and elsewhere
Bewley's Oriental Cafés have been a Dublin tradition for well over a century, and the Bewleys have been one of the city's best-known Quaker families. They began as tea and coffee merchants in Sycamore Street some time before 1842, and the idea of opening cafés sprang from the insistence of customers on sampling the products before purchase. The retail side of the business continues.

The cafés are in Grafton Street, South Great George's Street and Westmoreland Street, with smaller outlets elsewhere. They are noted for their old-world atmosphere and appearance. Particularly striking are the façades in Grafton Street— where mahogany and mosaics are oddly juxtaposed—and Westmoreland Street, recently but imaginatively rebuilt after a fire.

Bewley's emerged under new management from a financial crisis in 1986. The cafés and shops, however, retain most of their traditional charm.

Chester Beatty's collection included the 200 panels which were used to make the Chinese room (ceiling, left), as well as artefacts (inset)

BLUECOAT SCHOOL

Blackhall Place
The school, now occupied by the Incorporated Law Society, is a splendid Palladian building by Thomas Ivory, built in 1773–83; the cupola was added in 1904. The boardroom is noted for a fine plaster ceiling (1778–80) by Charles Thorp, though some of it is later, repair work.

The school was founded in 1669 in nearby Queen Street and granted a royal charter in 1670 by Charles II. Between the time it moved into the Blackhall Place building a century later until it vacated it in 1970 for a site outside the city, it was variously called the Bluecoat School, King's Hospital School and Bluecoat Boys' Hospital, but its formal title was Hospital and Free School of King Charles II. Its uniform of a navy blue cut-away brass-buttoned coat with navy blue knee breeches, yellow waistcoats, long yellow stockings and silver shoe buckles was only discarded for something less flamboyant in 1923. The choirboys still wear scarlet cassocks.

The ground at the back of the building, formerly a playing field, is the last surviving part of Oxmantown Green, once the central feature of a large Viking settlement.

Known for 250 years by their yellow stockings, the Bluecoat Schoolboys used this building until 1970

BOTANIC GARDENS

See National Botanic Gardens (page 48).

BRAZEN HEAD HOTEL

Bridge Street
This four-storey hostelry with its sunken courtyard is Dublin's oldest inn. It was constructed in about 1666, but seems to have been built on the site of a much older establishment, and its foundations certainly predate the 17th century. Visitors will notice that it is built at a lower level than its surroundings.

In James Joyce's *Ulysses*, Stephen Dedalus is told that 'you get a decent enough do in the Brazen Head over in Winetavern Street for a bob', a rare example of the expatriate Joyce, writing from memory, placing something in the wrong street.

Irish patriots Robert Emmet, Wolfe Tone, Henry Grattan, Daniel O'Connell and William Smith O'Brien were all patrons of the Brazen Head. The revolutionary United Irishmen regularly met in it, and some of their leaders were arrested here in 1797. A desk used by Emmet, who stayed in the inn, stood for many years in a corner of the bar, but was later moved to an upstairs room.

CASINO, MARINO

Malahide Road
The Casino stands in what was part of the grounds of the now-demolished Marino House. It was built in 1758 from a plan by Sir William Chambers and has been called one of the world's most perfect Palladian buildings. The original furniture has long gone but the structure was extensively restored by the Office of Public Works in the early 1980s and may be visited daily in summer and at winter weekends.

Surrounded by twelve Tuscan columns, eight in the four porticoes and four at the corners, it is based on Palladio's idea of the symmetrical villa and incorporates his notion of a temple façade running all around a building. Lions guard the approaches, and the graceful urns adorning the roof are outlets for a central heating system in the walls, operated by lighting fires in the grates. The building's ornate fireplaces and the jasper inlays in its doorstep indicate the opulence Lord Charlemont had in mind when he had it built as a 'pleasure-house', and wine cellars running off the surrounding basement area hint at convivial evenings. Balustrades, pediments and festooned panels hide the top storey, and the free-standing

'You get a decent enough do in the Brazen Head,' wrote Joyce, who placed it in Winetavern Street

columns and urns stress the mathematical precision.

Marino Crescent, at the bottom of Malahide Road, was built in 1792 by a painter named ffolliott, enemy of Lord Charlemont, to block the sea view. Bram Stoker, author of *Dracula*, was born here at No 15 in 1847.

CHESTER BEATTY LIBRARY AND GALLERY OF ORIENTAL ART

20 Shrewsbury Road
This contains the collection of Sir Alfred Chester Beatty, mining engineer and philanthropist, and comprises not only an outstanding assembly of books, including many 14th- and 15th-century French volumes, but a large number of paintings, papyri, bindings, wall hangings, costumes, carvings, drawings, Babylonian clay tablets and other artefacts illustrating the history of humanity from 2700BC to the present. The collection of Islamic material is particularly fine, and the huge array of Japanese prints, including several hundred *surimono*, is one of the best of its kind.

Opened to the public in 1954, the library and gallery can be visited all day Tuesday to Friday, and on Saturday afternoons.

The building's central section was erected around the ceiling of the Chinese Room, which is made up of 200 panels from an ancient temple. The Garden Room, with its illuminated Persian manuscripts and Armenian Gospels, was a favourite haunt of Chester Beatty himself in his declining years. He had never been able to survey his collection properly before its display here, and even now the full collection cannot be shown all at once.

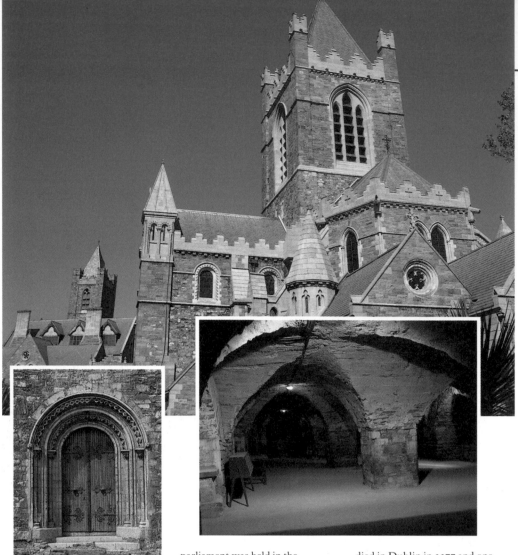

Christ Church, splendidly restored at the expense of distiller Henry Roe. The arch of the south door (above) is 12th-century, as is the crypt, used for taverns in the 16th century

CHRIST CHURCH CATHEDRAL

Christ Church Place
Christ Church, whose official name is the Cathedral of the Holy Trinity, replaced a timber church founded on the same site in 1038 by the Viking King Sitric. The cathedral is related in style to Glastonbury and Wells, and is, with St Patrick's, one of the best examples in Ireland of early Gothic architecture. Its large groin-vaulted crypt, crossing and transepts are its oldest parts, the crypt dating from 1172. Lambert Simnel, the Boy Pretender, was 'crowned' as King Edward VI of England here in 1487, using a crown borrowed from a statue of the Virgin Mary, possibly one which still exists in the Carmelite church in Whitefriar Street. In 1539 Archbishop Browne, flushed with the zeal of the Reformation, publicly burned relics here, which were said to include the staff of St Patrick, brought from Armagh; in 1559 a parliament was held in the cathedral and about 20 years later the nave had become a bazaar and there were taverns in the crypt.

Christ Church fell into such disrepair that its 1871–78 restoration involved considerable rebuilding. This was financed by distiller Henry Roe, and the architect was G E Street.

The nave
The interior of the Cathedral is extremely beautiful, an outstanding feature being the magnificent stonework of the nave and aisles. The nave was begun in 1213, its most westerly bay, different from the others, being built around 1234. It contains three prominent sarcophagi. One is that of a Bishop Lindsay who died in 1846, on whose land in Glasnevin the Holy Faith convent and schools were built. But controversy surrounds the two facing it across the church: the effigy of a recumbent knight with a smaller figure lying beside him. Some people maintain that they contain the remains of Strongbow, Anglo-Norman coloniser, and his son, whom he is said to have killed for fleeing from a battle. Others believe that they are the tombs of Strongbow and his consort Eva, while a third opinion insists that they have nothing to do with Strongbow at all. Strongbow, Earl of Pembroke, died in Dublin in 1177 and one school of thought maintains that his tomb, while certainly in this cathedral, cannot be identified since a roof fall in 1562.

The choir
The present choir dates from Street's restoration of the 1870s and resembles the pre-1350 one which he believed to be the original. Nonetheless he was attacked for 'destroying a 14th-century choir of unique interest', which Sir Richard Colt Hoare had called 'an unnatural medley of Gothic and Italian architecture'.

Exterior
In the grounds on the south side are ruins of the chapterhouse of an Augustinian priory which was attached to the cathedral until the Reformation. The arch of the cathedral's great south door is typically late 12th-century Norman. The new synod house across the road and the enclosed bridge over the top of the hill date only from Street's restoration, although the tower on the synod house is a remnant of the demolished medieval St Michael's Church. The tower on Christ Church itself is a 1330 construction. The cathedral's south wall was rebuilt by Street, who also added the flying buttresses on the north side.

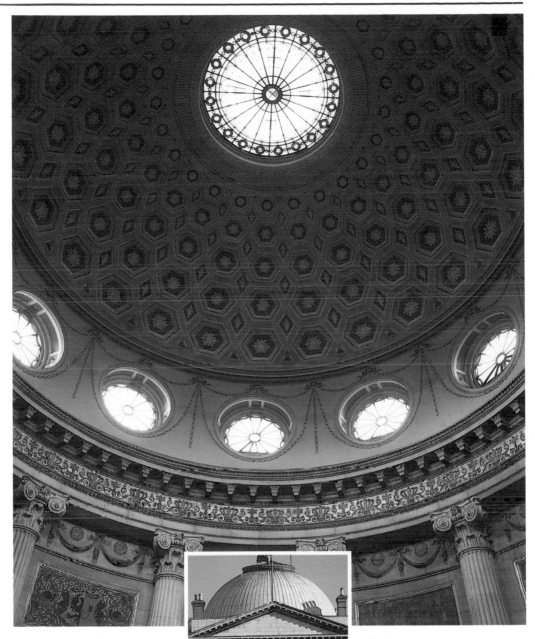

CITY HALL

Lord Edward Street
The first Earl of Cork had a mansion on this site, and later the Church of St Mary del Dame and a city gate called Dame's Gate stood here. The City Hall, with its fine six-columned Corinthian portico, closes the view up Parliament Street from the Liffey. This was the first street laid out by the Wide Streets Commission in the 18th century, when the bridge at its foot was the lowest on the river and the route from the north side to the parliament house led through it.

Thomas Cooley designed the City Hall (1769–79) as the Royal Exchange, and Thomas Ivory's 1781 municipal buildings above it were originally a bank. Inside the hall's balustrade, with its urns and four black trefoils of lamps, is an empty plinth. It was meant for a statue of Daniel O'Connell, who

City Hall: façade and central dome. One of the 102 royal charters stored inside this imposing building granted Dublin to Bristol, in 1171

included a spell as Lord Mayor of Dublin among his achievements. The statue, by John Hogan, is inside the building, as are marble statues of Thomas Davis, Dr Charles Lucas and Thomas Drummond, the latter also by Hogan. Lucas was an 18th-century apothecary in the city who advocated the reform of the Corporation and opposed attempts by the English parliament to impose its will on Ireland. He was praised as a pioneer of Irish liberty by Henry Grattan; his statue is by Edward Smyth. Drummond, a Scot, was an organiser of the Royal Irish Constabulary and an under-secretary at Dublin Castle from 1835. A fine marble statue of Henry Grattan by Sir Francis Chantrey is in a stairwell on the right.

The building's beautiful coffered dome is best viewed from inside the circular central hall. Municipal archives are stored in City Hall.

CIVIC MUSEUM

See Dublin Civic Museum (page 39).

CUSTOM HOUSE

Custom House Quay
One of Ireland's finest buildings, the Custom House is usually viewed from across the Liffey, and much of its exquisite detail is missed. It is 375ft long and 205ft deep, and its sides almost exactly face the principal compass points. The central front projection is joined to the end pavilions by arcades, each with seven arches, and all the columns along the building's front have harps in the capitals. The graceful copper dome, with its four pedimented clocks, brings the height to 120ft, and above this rises a 16ft figure of Hope, resting on her anchor.

Below the building's dividing frieze, 13 heads of riverine gods represent 13 Irish rivers. These form the keystones of arches. Over the main door a 14th head is a female representation of the Atlantic Ocean. Several bovine heads recall the port's beef trade. The four statues along the back of the building represent Europe, Asia, Africa and America. The building's back and side are of mountain granite, the front of Portland stone.

The building of the Custom House (1781–91) was opposed by local residents who feared that it

James Malton's view of the Custom House, 1793. On 25 May 1921 it was seized and later burnt; and although restored, it has needed more work since (damage detail, inset)

would make the area a slum, by commercial interests from an older custom house upriver and by the Dublin Corporation. Hired mobs pulled up piles and architect James Gandon often appeared on the site wearing his sword.

During fighting in 1921 the Custom House was burned to a shell, but it was rebuilt with all the glory of the original.

DUBLIN CASTLE

Cork Hill
King John ordered the building of Dublin Castle in 1204 as part of the city's defensive system. It was threatened by Edward de Bruce in 1317, besieged by Silken Thomas Fitzgerald in 1534 and was the scene of skirmishes in rebellions in 1803 and 1916. Red Hugh O'Donnell, Ulster chieftain, made celebrated escapes from its prison in 1591 and 1592. Now much rebuilt, it is a castle only in name.

In the upper yard, under the Bedford clocktower, was the 1552 genealogical office (see p. 74) with a Heraldic Museum from which the regalia called the Irish crown jewels were stolen in 1907.

State Apartments
These splendid apartments provided living quarters for the English Viceroys before the establishment of the Viceregal Lodge in the Phoenix Park. The grand staircase leads to the Battleaxe Landing, named after

ceremonial bodyguards' weapons. The Robert Adam-style carpets incorporate the arms of the four Irish provinces. To the left is St Patrick's Hall, with ceiling paintings by Vincenzo Valdre, galleries and gilt pillars. Its name derives from the Order of St Patrick, created in 1783, and the royal standard and colourful ones of 21 of the knights are displayed. The central painting is of George III, Britannia and Hibernia.

Next come the 15th-century Bermingham Tower and the circular supper room with a 19th-century brass chandelier. The shamrock, rose and thistle in its garland can be seen in the ceiling and carpet patterns, which are identical, representing the union of Ireland with England and Scotland. The beautiful, blue, oval Wedgwood room contains a Waterford glass chandelier, an Adam marble fireplace and Chinese-style Chippendale chairs. Also here are three paintings by Angelica Kaufmann, circular reproductions of 'Night' and 'Day' by Danish sculptor Berthel Thorwaldsen, a bust of Voltaire and four black Wedgwood panels by John Flaxman, who worked for the Wedgwood family. This room leads to George's Hall, in the castle's western extremity, which was built as a supper room for the visit of George V and Queen Mary in 1911. It has monochrome chiaroscuro paintings with a three-dimensional effect, by 18th-century Flemish artist Peter de Gree.

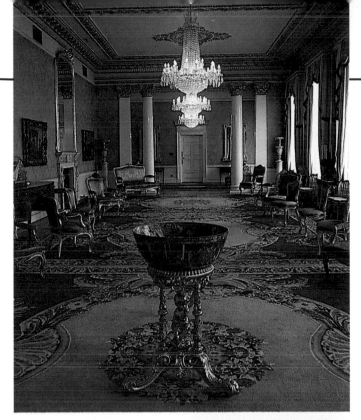

The picture gallery is east of here, and its Ionic columns show where it was originally divided into large and small dining rooms and a drawing room. It has portraits of Viceroys and chandeliers of Venetian glass.

Throne Room

Eastward again is the Throne Room with its heavy throne believed to have been presented by William of Orange, and a huge brass chandelier weighing more than a ton. The ovals and roundels on the walls are by the 18th-century Venetian Giambattista Bellucci.

Next is the State drawing room, which was badly damaged by fire in 1941, and restored in 1968 in the style of the 18th century. It has French silk upholstery, Waterford glass, paintings by Giovanni Panini on loan from the National Gallery and a 13th-century Chinese punchbowl adorned with wedding scenes. Next door, the square Apollo room has a 1746 plaster ceiling depicting the sun god. The room is a reproduction of the back drawing room (first floor) of Tracton House, and the ceiling and mantelpiece are the originals. Behind the drawing room and Apollo room is the State corridor designed by Edward Lovett Pearce, and across it are five bedrooms, two of them designated as 'king's' and 'queen's' and two of them with ceilings from the demolished Mespil House. The one called the Granard Room has a Van Dyck painting of Elizabeth, Countess of Southampton, Louis XV furniture and two solid marble Italian vases. The castellated stone wall which is visible across the castle garden from these rooms is said to have been built on Queen Victoria's orders to hide the backs

of the Stephen Street houses.

The State Apartments were used as a Red Cross hospital during World War I, and can be visited.

East of the bedrooms is the reconstructed Record Tower, one of the castle's original 13th-century corner towers and now one of its few fortress-like features. It houses documents and was a prison.

Chapel Royal

Below the Record Tower is Francis Johnston's Church of the Most Holy Trinity, formerly called the Chapel Royal. It opened on Christmas Day 1814. On its exterior are over 90 heads carved in Tullamore limestone by Edward Smyth and his son John. The church's plasterwork, with panels swept down to central clusters of cherubic heads, is by George Stapleton, and the carved oak panels by Richard Stewart, those in the gallery sides carrying the coats of arms of early Viceroys. Arms of later Viceroys are on stained glass in the gallery and on carved panels on the chancel walls. The stained glass in the four centre panels of the east window shows scenes from Christ's Passion.

The castle was handed over to the provisional Irish Government on 16 January 1922 by the last Viceroy, Lord Fitzalan.

DUBLIN CIVIC MUSEUM

South William Street
The exhibits here relate to the social history of the city, of which they give a compact overview. There are flint axes, coins from the Dublin Vikings' mint, prints, maps and regular thematic exhibitions. The large stone head labelled 'Nelson' is a remnant of the Nelson Pillar which stood in O'Connell Street until 1966, when it was blown up by extremists. It was a graceful Doric column by William Wilkins, with an internal 134-step spiral staircase, and had stood between Henry Street and North Earl Street since 1808.

In the fire-fighting section of the museum, a small goat cart is an inadequate memento of Hutton's coach-building firm in Summerhill, one of the most celebrated of such undertakings in Europe until early this century. Among its products was the Irish (Glass) Coach, bought by Queen Victoria at the Leinster Lawn exhibition in 1853, and still used by Queen Elizabeth II in Britain on State occasions. The fire section also displays the plaques of insurance companies, once placed on houses to guide the companies' own firemen to houses insured by them.

Fire insurance plaques (picture courtesy Dublin Civic Museum)

Fitzwilliam Square—'a remarkably high standard of finish'

ECCLES STREET

No 7 Eccles Street, home of Molly and Leopold Bloom in *Ulysses* was near Dorset Street where the newer part of the Mater Misericordiae hospital now stands. It was really the home of J F Byrne, friend of James Joyce and prototype of Cranly in *A Portrait of the Artist as a Young Man*. Its hall door was taken to the Bailey pub in Duke Street, and can still be seen there. No 63 was the 18th-century home of Sir Boyle Roche, celebrated clown of the Irish parliament. No 64, with its medallion copy of

No 64 Eccles Street

Michelangelo's *Moses*, was the home of architect Francis Johnston and later of Isaac Butt, founder of the Home Rule movement in 1870.

Eccles Street was planned as a radial arm of a huge circle of

detached mansions called Royal Circus. No new sponsor was found after Lord Mountjoy was killed in the 1798 Battle of New Ross, and the circus was never built. The older part of the Mater Misericordiae hospital (1852–61) is on part of its site.

Playwright Sean O'Casey was born in No 85 Upper Dorset Street (demolished), around the corner.

FINDLATER'S CHURCH

See Abbey Presbyterian Church (page 32).

FITZWILLIAM SQUARE

This quiet haven was the last of Dublin's Georgian squares to be completed, and is the only one whose central park is still reserved for residents. Its north side was begun in 1791, the west and east sides in 1798. Building was spasmodic, especially during the social decline which followed the 1800 Act of Union, and the square's last houses, on its south side, were not finished until 1825.

This square's houses are smaller and less ornate than those of the nearby Merrion Square, but the standard of finish is remarkably high. They first found favour with lawyers, but for many years now the square has been associated with the medical profession.

Fitzwilliam Square's construction was the final phase of a spate of Georgian building begun in 1762 by Viscount Fitzwilliam of Merrion, on the city end of his sprawling estates.

FOUR COURTS

Inns Quay
Dominating the upper quays as the Custom House does the lower, this great classical edifice is also the work of James Gandon. It took until 1802 to complete, partly because Gandon, fearing a revolution, went back to England for some time during the building. It has a 440ft river frontage and the central pile, 140ft square, is flanked by a pair of courtyards with screen

Parliament records and the originals of all Irish wills for 400 years were destroyed here in the 1922 shelling

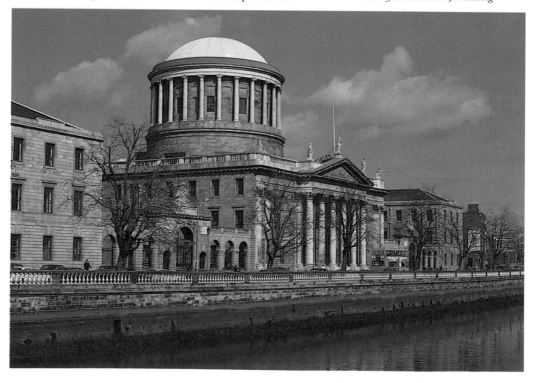

walls punctuated by triumphal arches.

The Four Courts were badly damaged by a bombardment in 1922 during the Civil War; restoration took nine years. The 64ft central dome is not a replica of the original, and purists complain that it rises too high.

The edifice was built to contain the Courts of Judicature, Chancery, King's Bench, Exchequer and Common Pleas. It is once again the home of the Irish Law Courts.

The Four Courts site was earlier occupied by the Abbey of St Saviour, a 1224 Dominican foundation, stones from which still exist in the surviving length of city walls at Cook Street. A tunnel ran under the Liffey from the Abbey to Christ Church and most of it still exists, though its ends have been long sealed up.

Father Mathew Bridge, just above the Four Courts, is on the site of the ford of hurdles which gave the city its Irish name of Baile Atha Cliath, and which was the crossing point of Sligh Cualann, the great road from Tara to Glendalough.

GAIETY THEATRE

South King Street
The yellow brick façade and ornate 'theatre baroque' interior have a special place in Dubliners' affections. The Gaiety, designed by C J Phipps for entrepreneur M Gunn and opened in 1871, was closely associated for many years with Jimmy O'Dea, most celebrated of all Dublin comics, who drew his audiences from all walks of life. Earlier Henry Irving, Beerbohm Tree, Ellen Terry and Martin Harvey all appeared here. It is noted for Christmas pantomimes, summer variety, seasonal appearances of the Dublin Grand Opera Society and the prestigious Rathmines and Rathgar Musical Society, as well as for other drama.

The Gaiety has survived more than one attempt to close it down and demolish it. Latterly it has been much used for televised shows and its suitability for this will probably ensure its survival.

GATE THEATRE

Cavendish Row
This building was designed as the New Assembly Rooms by Richard Johnston with advice from James Gandon, and built between 1784 and 1786 as part of the Rotunda

Cuchulainn in bronze in the GPO, regarded by many as the birthplace of the Free State. One of the world's most beautiful post offices, it is open usefully long hours, even on Sundays

complex. It became the Gate Theatre in 1929. The company had begun in 1928 as the Dublin Gate Theatre Studio in the Peacock, adjoining the Abbey Theatre, with four directors, Micheal MacLiammoir, Hilton Edwards, Madame Bannard Cogley and Gearoid O Lochlainn. The first public performance in the British Isles of Oscar Wilde's *Salome* was among its early productions.

The first production in Cavendish Row was *Faust*, opening on 17 February 1930. The Gate's early years were a financial struggle, with help coming from Lord Longford, who later became a director. As late as the 1950s he was to be seen outside the theatre with a collection box. The theatre now has an Arts Council grant.

Orson Welles and James Mason were among the actors who gained early experience at the Gate, which continues to stage avant garde productions, Irish and international.

GENERAL POST OFFICE

O'Connell Street
This massive building by Francis Johnston, completed in 1818, dominates Lower O'Connell Street and is always known by its initials. The 1916 Easter Rising began here with the reading of the Proclamation of the Irish Republic.

The Ionic portico of fluted columns is topped by John Smyth's figures of Hibernia with spear and harp, Mercury holding a purse, and Fidelity. Mortar marks still show where the royal arms formerly adorned the tympanum. On the façade, below a clock surmounted by a harp, the 1916 Rising is recalled. Inside, the main office's centrepiece is a bronze statue by Oliver Sheppard of the dying Cuchulainn, leader of the Red Branch Knights in Irish mythology, with a raven on his shoulder. Its green marble plinth carries the 1916 Proclamation and the names of its signatories.

The front of the GPO has for many years been the recognised site of reviewing stands for parades and of political and other rallies. In an arcade behind it is an official philatelic shop.

Despite survivals like this winch, the Grand Canal has been closed to commercial traffic since 1960. Its banks make delightful walking

GOVERNMENT BUILDINGS

Upper Merrion Street
Not to be confused with Leinster House, the main building here was designed by Sir Aston Webb as the Royal College of Science and opened by George V on his 1911 visit. Parts of it became offices of the Ministries of Agriculture and Local Government under the British administration, and the names of ministries can still be seen on scrolls held by carved cherubs with outsize crowns. The domed building has a rather gloomy ornate appearance, an Edwardian interpretation of the grand Georgian style. Notice that the heavy gate is dated 1922, marking the foundation of the new State.

Across the street the Department of Agriculture's Land Commission occupies Mornington House at No 24, generally recognised as the birthplace of the Duke of Wellington. (He is sometimes said to have been born in Trim, Co Meath.) Another of the house's occupants was Lord Castlereagh.

GRAFTON STREET

Grafton Street, once an 18th-century residential area, links St Stephen's Green and College Green and is still Dublin's most fashionable shopping street, despite some garishness in recent times. It is an exciting mixture of architectural styles, the shopfronts of Brown Thomas and Weir's being the most distinguished. Bewley's Café (see page 33) is a traditional meeting-place.

Reserved for pedestrians by day, after dark Grafton Street continues to be the centre of a fashionable area, due mainly to the pubs in the streets surrounding it, with their literary and other traditions. In Duke Street are The Bailey, and

Davy Byrne's 'moral pub' visited by Leopold Bloom in *Ulysses*. Harry Street has McDaid's, noted for its connections with author Brendan Behan and poet Patrick Kavanagh, and still something of a Bohemian haunt. In short Balfe Street, running from here to Chatham Street, Michael Balfe, composer of 'The Bohemian Girl', was born in 1808. In Chatham Street is Neary's, traditionally a theatrical gathering spot, with one of the finest pub fronts in the city.

GRAND CANAL

This 18th-century waterway, which connects Dublin Bay with the Shannon, curves through the city's inner southern suburbs to a harbour near the Liffey's mouth at Ringsend. Since its closure to commercial traffic in 1960 there have been regular proposals for filling it in, but it is a popular and a pleasant amenity, providing almost rural walks on its open banks. A particularly attractive part is the stretch from Leeson Street to Lower Mount Street, part of whose towpath is really rustic, as is the hump-backed Huband Bridge of 1791. Poet Patrick Kavanagh is recalled in a plaque here: he wrote about these 'leafy-with-love banks'.

The nine-bay Portobello House beside Portobello Bridge is a former canal hotel. It was designed in 1805 by Thomas Colbourne for those awaiting the early morning passenger barges which started from an adjacent harbour (now filled in). The canal benefited from the 18th-century building boom in Dublin, carrying thousands of tons of bricks from Tullamore and Pollagh in the midlands, but its passengers were never so lucrative.

Guinness Hop Store, Crane Street: displays and sampling for visitors

GUINNESS BREWERY

James's Street
Home of Dublin's best-known industry, at 60 acres this was until 1935 the world's largest brewery, and is still the largest stout-producing brewery.

Arthur Guinness founded his now world-famous business at St James's Gate on the south bank of the Liffey in 1759. He began brewing his own porter — nowadays known universally as stout — and campaigned successfully against a discrepancy in revenue rates which favoured imported brews. The oldest part of the brewery lies south of James's Street, behind a 200yd line of brick offices. The original St James's Gate spanned the street and was a gate into the outer city.

A branch of the Grand Canal was run specially into the brewery to enable the stout to be conveyed by barge to Limerick and Ballinasloe, and export consignments to the docks at Ringsend. In 1872 the brewery extended to the Liffey and acquired a fleet of ten colourful and much-loved river barges. The brewery still has a fleet of cross-channel ships, but its internal railway has gone. This had a corkscrew tunnel modelled on the Swiss St Gothard line, and some of its tracks are still

KILMAINHAM JAIL

Inchicore Road
Beside a granite courthouse which still carries the royal arms and has a pleasant garden at its side, the jail has become a shrine of Irish independence. Many political prisoners were detained here between 1796 and 1924, Eamon de Valera—later Taoiseach (prime minister) and then President—being among the last. Charles Stewart Parnell and Home Rule leader Isaac Butt were among the countless other patriots who spent some time in it. Its major significance, however, is that leaders of the 1916 Rising were executed here and this is what inspired the 1960s conversion of the derelict building into a museum, opened by de Valera in 1966.

Much voluntary labour and funds were expended on its restoration, which included a full replacement of the enormous roof. The jail, on the side of the small River Camac, has no aesthetic value. The chapel and cells may be inspected, as may exhibits relating to the prisoners; and the execution yard, which is a thick-walled gravelled quadrangle containing only an Irish flag on a staff and two timber crosses, is also on view. A plaque bears the names of Padraig Pearse, Sean MacDiarmada, James Connolly, Con Colbert and other executed nationalist leaders. Guided tours take place on Sunday afternoons.

to be seen outside the brewery. Guinness's is built on three levels, its biggest single buildings being the giant malt store and the fermentation building on either side of Market Street. The Guinness powerhouse is on the site of the absorbed Phoenix Brewery, once owned by Daniel O'Connell Jnr, son of the Irish patriot.

In 1800 Guinness was just one of 55 Dublin breweries. In this century its biggest Dublin rivals were D'Arcy's, downriver from it, and Watkins's, both now gone. The Watkins name lives on in Watkins's Buildings, constructed for its workers, a practice Guinness also followed.

Arthur Guinness's grandson, Sir Benjamin Lee Guinness, is remembered as the restorer of St Patrick's Cathedral. Sir Benjamin's son, Lord Ardilaun, opened St Stephen's Green to the public and laid it out as a park in 1880. He also rebuilt the Coombe maternity hospital in 1877, while his brother, Lord Iveagh, helped to finance a new wing of the Rotunda Hospital.

The visitors' centre in Crane Street is usually open on weekdays, with a film show and sampling of the product.

HUGH LANE GALLERY

See Municipal Gallery of Modern Art (page 46).

IVEAGH HOUSE

St Stephen's Green
This noble building forms Nos 80 and 81 on the south side of St Stephen's Green, and is occupied by the Department of Foreign Affairs. It was presented to the

State in 1939 by the 2nd Earl of Iveagh, a descendant of Sir Benjamin Lee Guinness, its third owner. Guinness had had the mansion, called Mountcashel House, thoroughly restored.

The neighbouring 18th-century houses, Nos 85 and 86, are both owned by University College. No 85, built in 1739 as Clanwilliam House by Richard Cassels, has fine plasterwork by Francini, including an exquisite Apollo panel in the later Louis XIV style. No 86, Newman House, formerly known as University House and St Patrick's House, was built in 1765 for Richard Whaley MP; soon afterwards it passed to his son 'Buck', a celebrated gambler and rake who became an MP at 18 and once walked from Dublin to Jerusalem to win a bet. The house has some notable plasterwork by Robert West.

Prisoners' cells can be inspected at Kilmainham Jail, re-opened in 1966 by President de Valera—a former inmate

KING'S INNS

Constitution Hill and Henrietta Street
A glorious classical edifice, built with many delays between 1795 and 1817 to the plans of James Gandon and his pupil Henry Aaron Baker, with some late flourishes by Francis Johnston. Its local nickname is 'the Temple'. Its fine library, founded in 1787, has over 100,000 volumes including a unique collection of English County histories, but is normally accessible only to members of the Inns. In the park, flanking the doors of the handsome dining hall and prerogative court, are figures of Ceres, goddess of food, a devotee of Bacchus, Law and Security by Edward Smyth.

The central courtyard joins the park and Henrietta Street, first of Dublin's Georgian streets, whose oldest houses date from 1720. It is now much decayed, but there has been some restoration of former tenements. It repays a visit, if only to see how these early Georgian mansions have much more variety in door styles and are also much larger than those that followed. The heavily-decorated doorway and façade of No 9, St Brigid's Hostel, were designed by Edward Lovett Pearce about 1730. Leading architect Richard Cassels designed houses here about the same time.

No 10, beside King's Inns, was the home of the Gardiners who laid out the street. The street's popularity with bishops led to the nickname 'Primate's Hill'.

LEINSTER HOUSE

Kildare Street
Now the meeting place of the Dail (lower house) and Seanad (senate) of the Irish Parliament, this mansion (1745–48) was the biggest and most lavish of the great town houses, and its erection greatly boosted development in this part of the city. Its first owner was Lord Kildare, who became Duke of Leinster in 1766. It stands on land formerly owned by the convent of St Mary de Hogge and later by the Molesworth family. The house's similarity to the Rotunda Hospital is no accident, as Richard Cassels used the same basic design for both, to save the hospital's founder unnecessary expense.

Leinster House backs on to Leinster Lawn, which Lord Kildare laid out on land leased from Viscount Fitzwilliam. An obelisk in the lawn's centre commemorates Michael Collins and Arthur Griffith, signatories of the 1921 Anglo-Irish Treaty, and Kevin O'Higgins, Minister for Justice in the first Dail. William Dargan, whose statue is at the lower end of the lawn near the National Gallery, was a railway builder who organised a great industrial exhibition here in 1853, for which Sir John Benson built a huge glass and steel structure similar to London's Crystal Palace. A statue of Prince Albert survives at the other end of the lawn, though a massive seated Queen Victoria figure of 1908 by John Hughes was removed from the Kildare Street side of Leinster House in 1948, amid amused comments.

Leinster House was sold in 1814 to the Royal Dublin Society, then simply the Dublin Society, by the Duke of Leinster. The society occupied it until the new parliament moved in during 1922, when the RDS moved to Ballsbridge. The public is admitted to the Dail visitors' gallery only with an introduction from a Teachta Dáil (MP).

LIBERTIES

This name applies to about 190 acres in the inner south-west area of the city and stems from a system founded under Magna Carta which gave some areas privileges and immunity from city jurisdiction in civil matters. Each such area had its own manor court. The areas now known as the Liberties are only some of the originals, but are those to which the name has adhered. They also include the districts in which many Huguenots, fleeing from France, settled from 1685 onward and engaged in weaving poplin, originally a fabric of pure silk and pure wool, on such a scale that Dublin became famous for it. A woollen industry followed, set up by manufacturers from England who brought the street names Spitalfields and Pimlico with them. Many Dutch and Flemish weavers moved in and Dutch-style weavers' houses survived in the area until the 1960s.

The Liberties area contains the two cathedrals (page 36 and 61), Marsh's Library (page 46) and many other places of interest. It also has Dublin's most famous 'flea market', the Iveagh Market in Francis Street, best visited on Saturdays when Thomas Street, Meath Street and Engine Alley come alive with smaller outdoor markets. The Augustinian Church in Thomas Street, with its huge spire, is a neo-Gothic essay by Pugin finished in 1874 and called by John Ruskin a 'poem in stone'. It stands on the site of an 1180 priory. A 150ft windmill tower further west, with a St Patrick weather-vane over its onion dome, is said to be the biggest such ever built in the British Isles. It is a remnant of Roe's distillery, the firm which restored Christ Church. There are two churches of St Nicholas Without (outside the walls) in this area, a classical Roman Catholic one in Francis Street better known as St Nicholas of Myra, and a Protestant one between Newmarket and the Coombe, built by the Huguenots in 1707.

George Bernard Shaw's birthplace (1856) is in the area, at 33 Synge Street.

MANSION HOUSE

Dawson Street
The Lord Mayor's official residence is somewhat over-ornate, with balustrade, wrought iron and glass canopy, and a line of eight tall lamps. The exterior paintwork disguises the fact that it is a brick building, built in the Queen Anne style in 1710 by Joshua Dawson, after whom this street is named. In 1715 the Corporation, deciding that the Lord Mayor needed a permanent residence, bought the house and its large surrounding garden from Dawson for £3500, with no rent payable after that, but 'one loaf of double refined sugar of six pounds weight' to be delivered every Christmas to Dawson's agents if demanded. The first Irish Parliament adopted the Declaration of Independence here in 1919.

The city arms surmount the façade, with the same motif on the side gate leading to the large Round Room behind the house. This room was built in 1821, at Corporation expense, for the reception of George IV. It has a stage and large gallery, and accommodates public meetings, Irish music festivals and exhibitions such as the August antiques fair.

Not all Lord Mayors choose to live in the Mansion House, as latterly a political arrangement has made it almost certain that their terms do not exceed a year.

MARINO

See Casino (page 35).

The Guinness windmill tower (below) is
a notable landmark in the area known as
the Liberties, where the visitor can also
find one of Dublin's most colourful scenes,
Iveagh Market (right).
Elegant Leinster House (left), viewed
from Leinster Lawn with its 1921
commemorative obelisk.
The city's coat-of-arms surmounts the
entrance to the Mansion House, where the
1921 peace treaty was signed (below left)

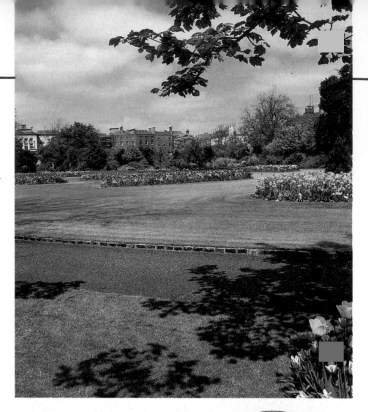

MARSH'S LIBRARY

St Patrick's Close
Narcissus Marsh, Archbishop of
Dublin, founded and endowed this
library in 1701; it was built to the
design of Sir William Robinson
and opened in 1707. It is the oldest
public library in Ireland. The
original cages into which readers
were locked to prevent stealing still
survive.

The collection's 25,000 books
include the personal library of
Stillingfleet, Bishop of Worcester,
who died in 1699, and Dean Swift's
annotated copy of Clarendon's
History of the Great Rebellion, and
there are about 200 manuscripts.
Marsh, who resigned as provost of
Trinity in 1683, died in 1713 and is
buried in St Patrick's Cathedral,
not far from his enemy Jonathan
Swift. Swift blamed Marsh for his
lack of promotion in the Church of
Ireland, and in 1710 wrote a
stinging pamphlet about the
archbishop.

The library is open most
weekdays.

MERRION SQUARE

The east side of this square and its
southward continuation comprised
Europe's longest unbroken stretch
of Georgian houses until a decision
by the Electricity Supply Board in
1961 to demolish 26 houses in
Lower Fitzwilliam Street and build
an office block. The square was
originally intended by Viscount
Fitzwilliam to run further east and
be much bigger than it is. John and
George Ensor finished the square's
north side in 1764, but its houses
have less grandeur than those
elsewhere. On the west side the
Rutland Fountain of 1791 is by
H A Baker, with urns from the
Wedgwood works in Staffordshire.

The central park was opened to
the public, without too much
artificial development, after a plan
to build a Roman Catholic
cathedral there was abandoned. No
39 on the east side was burned
down by extremists in the early
1970s but has been restored. On the
south side Daniel O'Connell lived
at No 56, Nobel prizewinning
physicist Erwin Schrodinger at
No 65, author Sheridan LeFanu at
No 70 and W B Yeats at No 82.
George Russell, Yeats's ally in the
Irish literary revival, had an office
at No 84. John Bowden's St
Stephen's Church (1824) to the east
is nicknamed the 'Peppercanister
Church'; it is a handsome building
with a Greek-style portico.

MOUNTJOY SQUARE

The only Georgian square in the
city which is literally a square, this
architectural set-piece has suffered
most from decay. Its south side was
worst hit, and restoration has taken
the form of 'façade Georgian' to a
large extent, with modern offices
behind simulated domestic fronts.
Houses on the square's north and
east sides have been either better
maintained or expensively restored.

The square was built (1792–
1818) on a plateau called Mountjoy
Fields, and was first called
Gardiner's Square. The site was
chosen for its height as this was
considered healthier. There is a
superb view across the city to the
mountains from the top back
windows of the southern houses. It
was intended to build St George's
Church (see page 58) in the middle
of the square's park, but the plan
was abandoned. Tradition says
Brian Boru pitched his tent here at
the Battle of Clontarf on 23 April
1014; the name Clontarf certainly
included this area then.

Playwright Sean O'Casey lived
at No 35 and set *The Shadow of a
Gunman* here, calling it Hilljoy
Square. Timothy Healy, first
Governor-General of the Irish Free
State, lived in No 1. In Fitzgibbon
Street, off the square, James Joyce
lived as a boy in No 14.

MUNICIPAL GALLERY OF
MODERN ART

Parnell Square North
Also known as the Hugh Lane
Gallery from the paintings of the
Hugh Lane Bequest which it
contains, the gallery is housed in
Charlemont House, built (1762–
65) for the Earl of Charlemont to
Sir William Chambers' design. It is

*The beauty of Merrion Square, where
Oscar Wilde lived at No 1 with his
father (above) and mother*

a five-bay mansion flanked by
curving screen walls with niches
and balustrades. Its fine interior is
often overlooked, being now a
background to works of art. The
Earl patronised the arts and
founded the Royal Irish Academy
in 1785; Samuel Johnson and
Joshua Reynolds were visitors to
Charlemont House.

As well as displaying art,
including modern art exhibitions,
the gallery has a regular
programme of classical and modern
musical events throughout the
year, the details being advertised in
the *Irish Times* on Saturdays.
Lectures on the collection and
other art subjects, with films and
slides, are given each Sunday at
noon. Art activities for children,
with materials supplied, are
conducted in the sculpture hall
each Saturday at 11.30 am. The
Municipal Gallery is financed and
run by Dublin Corporation.

Hugh Lane Bequest
This was the subject of a long-
running dispute between the
Municipal and the Tate Gallery,

Dolls on show at the Museum of Childhood (above). John's Miss Iris Tree *(below) is one of the fine works at the Gallery of Modern Art, where budding artists enjoy themselves in the sculpture hall (bottom)*

London, about where the bequest paintings should be hung. The paintings which eventually came to Dublin are not grouped together in the gallery, but are individually ascribed, in amongst Manet's *Eva Gonzalez*, Monet's *Lavacourt Winter*, Augustus John's *A Boy in Brown* and *Miss Iris Tree*, Robert Gregory's *Coole Lake*, Antonio Mancini's portrait of Lady Gregory, Courbet's *The Pool*, Boudin's *The Beach, Tourgeville* and *At the Seaside* and works by Corot, Orpen, Wilson Steer, Mark Fisher (*The Bathers*) and Walter Osborne's *The Fish Market, Patrick Street, Dublin*, a work which captures the essence of old Dublin.

Other Exhibits
Modern sculpture takes a central place in the gallery. Niki de Saint Phalle's *Big Bird* is here, as are Henry Moore's *The Piper* and once-controversial *Reclining Figure*.

To their left a side room contains portraits, landscapes and waterscapes by Frank O'Meara, John Lavery, Sidney Nolan, Roderic O Connor (*A Breton Girl*), J J Shannon, Albert Moore, Ernest Quost and one Millais, *Lilacs*. More modern work by Patrick Scott, Patrick Hall, Anthony Greene, Cecil King, Erik van de Grijn, Patrick Harris, George Dokoupil and Patrick Ireland (his striking, mirrored *Ogham*) are in the room behind the Moore sculpture, and behind that again are many Constables and works by Degas, George Clausen and others, including the charming *Tea Party*

of H Bellingham Smith.

Further back, a room with a heavy Lane Bequest content and dominated by *Eva Gonzalez*, also houses work by Corot, Morisot, J J Fourain, Norman Garstin and Raimundo de Madrazo. The back section of a long room at the gallery's right is more impressionistic in content and contains Louis le Brocquy's *Child in a Yard*, works by Mary Swanzy, Edward McGuire, Nano Reid, Paul Henry, Patrick Tuohy, W J Leech, Norah McGuinness (*Garden Green*) and Maurice MacGonigal, together with Jack B Yeats's powerful seascape *There is no Night*. Also here are a William Orpen self-portrait, John Lavery's portrait of patriot Arthur Griffith and John Keating's fine portrait *The Tipperary Hurler*.

MUSEUM OF CHILDHOOD

20 Palmerston Park
In the pleasant southern suburb of Rathmines, this repository of childhood delights is a charming experience. Its main attraction is a collection of dolls dating from the early 18th century, many of them beautifully dressed, some valued in four figures because of their rarity. There are also toy prams and other playthings, doll's houses and their miniature furniture of varying antiquity, and a selection of rocking horses. The best way to visit it is in the company of at least one small child.

The museum is open on Sundays and most summer days.

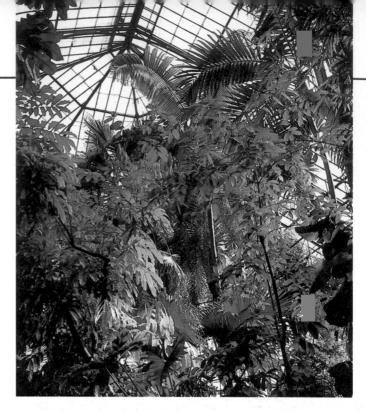

The cast-iron Palm House at the National Botanic Gardens

NATIONAL BOTANIC GARDENS

Botanic Road, Glasnevin
The Gardens were founded here in 1795 by Professor Walter Wade of the Dublin Society (later RDS). They came under State control in 1878, when they were already quite famous. They now occupy over 50 acres, and while their main purpose remains to promote the study of horticulture and botany they have for many years been a retreat for a public in search of beauty and tranquillity. The Gardens have about 20,000 species and varieties, and are open daily.

Glasnevin's contribution to botanical history includes the first reported attempt to raise orchids from seed (1844), the first successful hybridisation of the insectivorous pitcher-plants (1870) and the introduction to European gardens of pampas grass and giant lilies.

Main Walk
Just left of the main entrance, the Thomas Moore Rose is descended from the rose which inspired Moore's 'The Last Rose of Summer'. The superintendent's house, to the right, has one of the few thornless climbing roses in the British Isles. The Main Walk begins at a low greenhouse which contains the cactus and the succulent, aquatic and fern sections. In summer the aquatic section has giant Amazon water-lilies on its pool. *Todea Barbara*, the Gardens' oldest plant, estimated at nearly 400 years old, is in the fern section.

The walk passes beside the Curvilinear Range of greenhouses (1843) on the right, among the oldest curved glass conservatories in the world. (The oldest, from the same builder, Richard Turner of Ballsbridge, Dublin, is in Belfast's botanic gardens; Turner also built a huge palm house in London's Kew Gardens.) On the far side of the walk is the Palm House of 1884. Next comes a junction, with slow-growing conifers straight ahead and a charming rockery on the right; the Yew Walk or Addison Walk beyond it is sheltered by very old trees, since this, the oldest part, was planted over 50 years before the Gardens opened. It was a haunt of essayist Joseph Addison. Beyond it an area of conifer and beech slopes down to the River Tolka and its mill-race, where are magnolia, cypress and the Chinese Tulip tree. Between the Addison Walk and the mill-race is a splendid tall Sierra redwood. Corsican, Scots and Monterey pine are also here.

Straight ahead are wide areas of ash, lime, maple, yew, larch, elm, holly, hawthorn, beech, hickory, alder, hazel, hornbeam, eucalyptus and other trees.

Herbaceous Border
South-east from the junction to the palm house runs the very lovely (in season) Herbaceous Border, with oak and cedar on its right, and beyond that the vegetable garden, herb and lawn gardens, native plants and poisonous plants. The Students' Walk behind the palm house has representatives of the more important plant families. The Chinese shrubbery is near the herb garden.

Greenhouses
The Curvilinear Range contains a huge variety of indoor plants and flowers. More exotic is the Palm House with its tall central tropical tree collection and wings for camellias, flowering pot plants and orchids. Small bananas grow in the steamy atmosphere here.

Roses
The rose garden with its sundial is in the north-east corner of the Gardens beyond the Tolka. A visit repays the walk.

NATIONAL CONCERT HALL

See University College Dublin (page 66)

NATIONAL GALLERY OF IRELAND

Merrion Square West
The gallery building (1859–64) is by Francis Fowke, architect of London's Victoria and Albert Museum and Edinburgh's Royal Scottish Museum. Some additions, including the rather forbidding porch, are by Sir Thomas N Deane. Paintings assembled for the 1853 Leinster Lawn exhibition formed the nucleus of the gallery's collection. Today the collection contains over 2200 paintings,

almost 5000 watercolours and drawings, 250 pieces of sculpture, and the Hunt Bequest of vestments and *objets d'art*. A room is devoted to American painting and there is an important display of icons.

Ground Floor
Room 1A contains Italian Primitives and icons, including di Paolo's *The Crucifixion*, Ucello's *Virgin and Child* and Fra Angelico's *Martyrdom of Ss Cosmos and Damian*. Also here is *The Virgin and Child Hodigitria* (c.1325) from the Constantinople School.

Rooms 2–7 contain the Irish School, with works by James Latham, Nathaniel Hone, James Barry, George Barrett, Thomas Roberts, Francis Danby, Daniel Maclise, Walter Osborne, Jack B Yeats and others. Notable are Osborne's *St Patrick's Close, Dublin* (1887), showing fish stalls in a vanished streetscape, and Hone's *The Conjuror*, which caused a

The National Gallery was founded by William Dargan, organiser of the 1853 Exhibition. Emil Nolde's Women in the Garden *is a striking exhibit*

scandal in 1775, its painted-out nudes still visible in X-rays.

The French School is in Rooms 28 and 30, artists represented including Degas, Monet, Corot, Poussin, Millet, Chardin, H Robert, David, Sisley and Delacroix. Degas's *Ballet Girls* (1886) is among the exhibits.

Upstairs
The Italian School continues in Rooms 9, 10, 11, 12 and 13, with works by Titian, Tintoretto, Veronese, Perugino, Moroni, Lanfranco, Maratta, Castiglione, Strozzi (a charming *Summer and Spring*), Guardi, Canaletto, Panini and Batoni. Works by leading English masters, in Rooms 15–17, include *The Dublin Volunteers in College Green* by Wheatley, Reynolds's amazing *The Earl of Bellamont*, Hogarth's evocative *The Mackinnon Children*, and paintings by Gainsborough, Stubbs, Wilson and Landseer.

Other Schools
In the Spanish room, El Greco, Murillo, Ribera, Goya and Zubaran are represented; Murillo's *The Holy Family* is notable. In the Dutch School, Rooms 36 and 37, there is a fine collection of minor masters, plus works by Rembrandt, Jan Steen, Jan van Goyen, the van Ruisdaels, Peter Clacsz, Pieter de Hooch and Emanuel de Witte.

Admirable examples of early Flemish art are in Rooms 21 and 35, along with later works by Rubens and Van Dyck. The German School (Room 34) has works by Wolfgang Huber, Georg Pencz and Lucas Cranach (Elder), and *The Apostles Bidding Farewell* by an unknown artist of the 15th-century Styrian (Austrian) School.

In Room 22 the American School is well represented by Whistler, John Singer Sargent, Gilbert Stuart and Benjamin West.

The gallery has a bookshop and restaurant.

NATIONAL LIBRARY

Kildare Street
The Library is to the left as one faces Leinster House, and was designed by Sir Thomas Newenham Deane and his son Sir Thomas Manly Deane and built in 1884–1890. Its pavilion and semi-circle of columns are matched in the National Museum facing it, also the work of the Deanes. The Library was the brainchild of the Royal Dublin Society.

It is a treasure-house of information about Ireland, not only in the huge number of books but in magazines and newspapers, many of whose files are complete since publication began. There is also a comprehensive photographic archive. Tickets are needed for reading books, and latterly visitors have been referred for some services to a newer library in the Ilac Centre, Henry Street, so would-be visitors should phone to enquire about access.

NATIONAL MUSEUM

Kildare Street
The Museum, facing the National
Library, was completed in 1890.
The main room in the ground floor
is devoted to Irish antiquities.
There is a Viking sub-section of
weapons, personal adornments,
hunting, fishing, digging and
domestic implements and human
remains. There are earlier Roman
brooches and pins, either imported
or the property of refugees from
Brigantia, a Roman colony in
northern England, and a 52ft dug-
out canoe, unearthed in Co Galway
in 1902. From the Iron Age are
Ogham and other carved stones,

*National Gallery treasures: the Ardagh
silver chalice, with gold decoration, and
the 12th-century processional Cross of Cong*

weapons, cooking implements,
gold and bronze ornaments
including gold collars and bronze
'*crotals*', rare and unique to Ireland,
resembling modern grenades and
containing pebbles which were
used as musical instruments or
possibly part of a cult of the bull.
From the Bronze Age are daggers,
swords, tools, beads, necklaces and
garrotte-like gold torques.

Glass, Lace and Music
The visitor going up a staircase
displaying early 18th-century
embroidery, with 15th-century
Mass vestments on the landing,
will find lovely 18th- and 19th-
century glass from Dublin,
Waterford, Cork and England, as
well as 16th-, 17th- and 18th-
century Venetian, 18th- and 19th-
century Persian and Indian and
some medieval Eastern glass. The

*The Tara brooch, a masterpiece of
delicate 8th-century workmanship*

Egyptian sand-core glass dates
from 700 – 100BC. There is much
exquisite 19th- and early 20th-
century lace.

Also here are exquisite 17th- and
18th-century Dublin gold and
silver, many old optical and
measuring instruments, 18th-
century pianos, guitars and
harpsichords, and 17th- and 18th-
century harps, including that of
Turlough O'Carolan. A parade of
dress from 1750 onwards is rather
oddly continued at the bottom of
the gallery stairs, beside 18th- and
19th-century dolls.

Presidential Room
This room contains items
associated with all of Ireland's
presidents, including gifts from
foreign heads of State and
documents. Its most curious
exhibit is part of a heat shield from
the 1969 moon landing mission,
presented to President de Valera.

1916 Rising
Weapons, documents and personal
effects from the 1916 Rising and
later War of Independence have a
downstairs room to themselves.
Here are pistols belonging to
Padraig Pearse and Countess
Markievicz, Pearse's barrister wig,
gown and swordstick, James
Connolly's blood-stained shirt, the
military overcoat and cap worn by
Michael Collins at the time of his
shooting in 1922, uniforms, flags
and banners. In a room behind this
are 19th-century uniforms worn by

Thomas Davis and William Smith O'Brien, and Land War banners.

Treasury

The Museum's Treasury, also downstairs, has an entrance charge which includes admission to a 20-minute film. Among its prized items are the 8th-century Ardagh silver chalice and 9th-century Derrynaflan chalice, placed in adjacent cases for comparison. The second of these is a 1980 find, and its ownership has already been the subject of a celebrated court case. Here, too, are the 8th-century Tara brooch, 8th-century Derrynaflan paten, 1st-century BC Broighter hoard, 2nd-century AD Petrie crown, 12th-century Cross of Cong, 5th- to 8th-century St Patrick's Bell and 12th-century Clonmacnoise crozier.

The natural history section, across Leinster Lawn from the National Gallery, has a large collection of animals, birds and fish, both Irish and general. Due to age, some skin colours are not original. The museum has another section, in Merrion Row, used for special exhibitions.

NEWMAN HOUSE

See Iveagh House (page 43).

A 12ft bronze statue of the Liberator crowns the O'Connell monument

O'CONNELL STREET

O'Connell Bridge (1880) replaced James Gandon's narrower Carlisle Bridge of 1794. It is overlooked by John Henry Foley's 1854 bronze figure of Daniel O'Connell in the base of which can be seen the arms of the Irish provinces and 30 figures by Foley, the central one, with harp, representing Hibernia. The four big winged figures, often miscalled angels, are the four Victories, representing Courage,

19th-century stained glass, one reminder of the Olympia's former glory

Eloquence, Fidelity and Patriotism as qualities of the Liberator. The bullet hole in the right breast of the Victory facing the Ulster Bank occurred during fighting some time between 1916 and 1922. Above this monument is one to William Smith O'Brien, a nationalist who survived a death sentence imposed for treason in 1848. Following are figures of Sir John Grey, 19th-century civic administrator and newspaper owner, and James Larkin, labour leader famed for organising the general strike of 1913. Half-way up the street is the site of the erstwhile Nelson Pillar (see Dublin Civic Museum, page 39). Above this is a statue of the noted temperance crusader Fr Mathew, erected in 1890 as a centenary memorial. At the top of the street the Charles Stewart Parnell monument has a symbolic flame atop an obelisk of polished pink granite and a bronze statue (by Dublin-born Augustus Saint-Gaudens) of Parnell, the patriot, whose affair with Kitty O'Shea brought his downfall.

The street is 150ft wide. Its upper part was formerly a Georgian boulevard, Gardiner's Mall, which began the tradition of trees in the street centre. This half of the street lacks public buildings and is dominated by the Gresham Hotel and two large cinema complexes, while the Ambassador cinema facing down it is the rebuilt Round Room of the Rotunda Hospital complex.

Behind the street's upper west side is Moore Street, Dublin's colourful open-air food market, a place of real character.

The lower half of the street is dominated by the GPO (see entry, page 41). The entire street was largely rebuilt after the 'Troubles'. The Ulster Bank, for example, looks Victorian but is dated 1923. There have been many later

changes; several more cinemas have come and gone. Some of the development was regrettable, but it was not until the late 1980s that a special commission was set up to tighten the rules for shopfronts and other displays and restore the street's old glory.

OLYMPIA THEATRE

Dame Street

The city's second oldest theatre, this became its biggest when the huge Theatre Royal in Hawkins Street, Europe's largest, was demolished in 1962. The Olympia's interior epitomises the old music hall style. It began, indeed, as the Star of Erin music hall in 1879, but was always popularly known as 'Dan Lowry's', after its owner. In 1897 it became the Empire Palace; a few years later the name changed again. Marie Lloyd, Gertie Gitana, George Formby, John Gielgud, Noel Coward, Alec Guinness, Gladys Cooper, Peggy Ashcroft, Tyrone Power, Margaret Rutherford and Laurel and Hardy have all performed here, as well as singer Victoria de Los Angeles, which indicates the variety of its past productions.

The theatre has a history of financial difficulty. It closed for some months in 1964, and ten years later the proscenium arch collapsed during a performance of *West Side Story*. The renovation fund-raising involved top Irish actors Micheal MacLiammoir and Siobhan McKenna in public appeals. Then, and again in 1987, performers gave their services free in a 'Save the Olympia' campaign. But it has survived and has resisted at least two attempts to demolish it.

PHOENIX PARK

This enclosed space has a circumference of about seven miles and an area of 1,752 acres, bigger than the combined area of London's Hyde Park, Regent's Park, St James's Park, Green Park, Kensington Gardens and Hampstead Heath. It contains gardens, lakes, woods, extensive playing areas for soccer, Gaelic football, hurling and camogie, a polo course, a cricket club, the second zoological gardens to be opened to the public in Europe, as well as the residences of the Irish President and US Ambassador, the headquarters of the Department of Defence, the police force and the Ordnance Survey, and a deer herd.

The park was walled by the Duke of Ormonde in 1671 and opened to the public in 1747 by Lord Chesterfield, the Lord Lieutenant, after whom its main road, running straight for over two miles, was named. The name Phoenix comes from 'fionn uisce', Irish words meaning clear water, inspired by a chalybeate spring which is now inside the zoo. The Phoenix Park racecourse is immediately outside the park.

Inside the Parkgate Street entrance, on the right, are the attractive People's Gardens, laid out in 1864. Further on is an intersection where John Henry Foley's equestrian statue of Lord Hugh Gough, distinguished Irish general, was blown up in 1944, repaired and destroyed by a second blast in 1957. On the right after the

Hollow, with its bandstand, is the zoo, with the long building and parade ground of the garda (police) headquarters in the distance.

Dublin Zoo
The Zoological Gardens opened in 1831 with an enclosure of 5½ acres, little more than a sixth of its present size. It still has an 1833 ticket office. The excellent layout was designed by Decimus Burton, architect to the Zoological Society of London. The society administering it became the Royal Zoological Society of Ireland in 1837 when Queen Victoria became its patron. Today it maintains its large collection of animals through admission,charges, subscriptions and commercial sponsorship. It is administered by a council which meets after formal breakfasts, a

tradition of which is that porridge is consumed standing up.

Dublin Zoo is one of the few places in the world where lions will breed in captivity, and over 700 of them have been bred here since 1857. One Dublin lioness mothered 75 cubs in 12 years. A lion from here achieved 'stardom' as the MGM film lion. The zoo includes many birds and a reptile house. Its most celebrated inmate has been a tuatera lizard with a socket under its skin for a third eye. A Haida Indian totem pole, presented to the State by the Canadian Government in 1970, is in the American black bears' enclosure, chosen as a vandal-free site. In a small area of crowned cranes beyond the sealions' pool, a wooden arrow marks the site of the spring which gave the park its 'Phoenix' name.

Two inmates of Europe's second zoo to be opened to the public

The zoo contains a lake, restaurants and a members' bar, and is open every day of the year.

Aras an Uachtarain
From the Polo Grounds (1870s) flanking the zoo a short road runs back to the elm-lined main road and a more open landscape. On the right, further out, is Aras an Uachtarain, the Presidential residence, built in 1751, enlarged in 1782 and added to again by Francis Johnston in the 1800s. It was then the Viceroy's residence; when the Irish Free State was founded the house was occupied by Governors-General until the office of President was created under the 1937 Constitution.

The most dramatic incident in the park's history took place on the main road opposite this house on 6 May 1882, when Lord Frederick Cavendish, Chief Secretary for Ireland, and his Under-Secretary, T H Burke, were assassinated by a secret society called the National Invincibles; five men were hanged for the crime.

The Phoenix Monument on its elaborate pedestal was erected by Lord Chesterfield in 1747; it is more often called the 'Eagle' monument since the flames which identify the fabled bird are not obvious in the grey stone. Away to the left are the 'Fifteen Acres', an area of football and hurling pitches really about 200 acres. A road skirting them goes to the American Ambassador's residence, formerly that of the murdered Cavendish. Beyond it is Oldtown Wood.

Forking left at the crossroads, a path leads out through White's Gate to the 1835 Castleknock College, in whose grounds is the ruin of Castleknock Castle. Before the college comes Farmleigh, Lord Iveagh's residence, where EEC Foreign Ministers met in 1975. Past Quarry Lake with its island, a path on the right leads to a house with a private theatre built by Luke Gardiner in 1728. Subsequently a cavalry barracks, since 1825 it has been the Ordnance Survey office. At the next crossroads, the right-hand road goes to the 1864 Mount Sackville convent and school. Straight ahead are the Glen Lake and Furry Glen in one of the park's most attractive parts. St Mary's Hospital, a Cheshire Home, occupies some buildings of the former Royal Hibernian Military School (1766), which was added to by Thomas Cooley (a handsome chapel, 1771) and Francis Johnston and had an 18-acre farm where the girls and boys worked.

Phoenix Park is an important centre for sport in Dublin, and the 1870 Polo Ground is one of several specially designated playing areas. The Phoenix Monument (left) is mid-18th-century

Magazine Fort
On the right is Chapelizod village, where Joseph Sheridan LeFanu lived and set his novel *The House by the Churchyard*. From here a path winds past trees along Corkscrew Hill to St Thomas's Hill and its grim deserted Magazine Fort, which took from 1735 to 1801 to complete. It stands on the site of a house where Oliver Cromwell's son Henry and a Lord Falkland had lived. This fort was raided in 1916 by insurgents and again in 1939 by the IRA.

The road leads between the Wellington Monument to the right and to the left the army athletic grounds, cricket grounds and Citadel Pond, better known as the Dog Pond. The Phoenix Cricket Club of 1830 is the second-oldest surviving cricket club in Ireland. The Wellington Monument, 205ft to the top of its obelisk, stands over 11 sloping steps, the bottom one being 480ft square. Designed by Robert Smirke, it was built between 1817 and 1861, and may be the world's tallest obelisk. An inscription on its huge base reads:
Asia and Europe, saved by thee, proclaim
Invincible in war thy deathless name;
Now round thy brow the civic oak we twine
That every earthly honour may be thine

POWERSCOURT HOUSE

South William Street
This stately town house of the
Powerscourt family, whose major
estate was in Enniskerry, Co
Wicklow, was built in 1771 to the
design of Robert Mack, who had
earlier planned Essex—now
Grattan—Bridge, linking Capel
Street and Parliament Street. The
mansion later became an
anachronism, boxed in by
commercial streets, but by then it
had changed hands, being sold to a
wholesale clothing and textile firm
as early as 1835 and remaining with
them for well over 100 years. Its
excellent plasterwork by Michael
Stapleton survived this commercial
use.

In the 1980s the tall house and its
large galleried courtyard running
back towards Clarendon Street
were converted to the Powerscourt
Townhouse Centre, of mainly
small, select shops and restaurants,
on the lines of a shopping mall but
more intimate and sophisticated.
The result has been to link the
shopping hub of Grafton Street via
narrow Johnston's Court with the
arcade of the South City Market in
South Great George's Street,
hitherto somewhat neglected, and
create a long, very varied and
charming traffic-free precinct. The
palatial redbrick building over the

*The transformation of Powerscourt
House into a shopping centre is a triumph
of enlightened development*

market arcade (1892) is a happy
coincidence. Henry II once built a
palace here.

PRO-CATHEDRAL

Marlborough Street
Designed by amateur architect
John Sweetman of Raheny,
Dublin, the church's façade with its
six-pillared Doric portico is a copy
of the Temple of Theseus in
Athens; the Renaissance interior is
modelled on the Church of St
Philip de Reule in Paris. St Mary's
Pro-Cathedral was built between
1815 and 1825 on the site of a
mansion of Lord Annesley. It had
been decided to build it in
O'Connell Street where the GPO
now is, but that plan was
abandoned from fear of official
opposition; yet the design is far
more suitable to the original site, as
in narrow Marlborough Street one
has to go some distance into the
grounds of the Department of
Education across the road to
appreciate the great spread of the
façade and see the dome.

In the apse are two altars with
mosaics and a memorial window to
Sir James Power, a chairman of

*The Pro-Cathedral also contains a
magnificent white marble altar*

Power's Distillery. The church is
used by Catholics for the religious
services which accompany some
State occasions, usually with a
corresponding service being held
in St Patrick's Cathedral.

The street corner above the
church on the opposite side of
Marlborough Street marked one
edge of 'Monto', a red light district
of the early 1900s, written about by
Joyce and St John Gogarty and
called by *Encyclopaedia Britannica* in
those days more blatant 'even than
Algiers'.

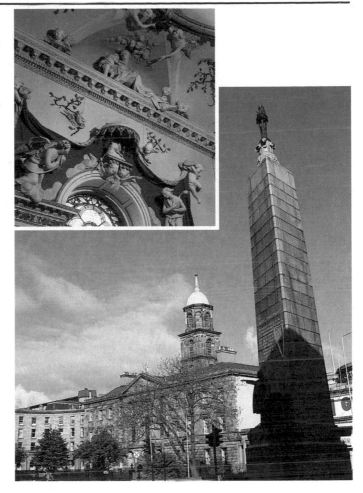

PROSPECT CEMETERY

Glasnevin
The cemetery wall on the right of Finglas Road coming from the town still has the watch-towers which were once manned by armed guards to deter body-snatchers. The cemetery has spread from its original nine acres to over 100. Burials and cremations are not confined to members of any one religious persuasion, although it was opened in 1832 for the burial of Catholics, as Catholic burial services had run into opposition elsewhere in the city. Below the cemetery the road fork at Hart's Corner is divided by a narrower road leading to an old gate of the graveyard. This gate, long closed, was opened at the suggestion of Daniel O'Connell to avoid a turnpike on Finglas Road at which funerals had to pay tolls.

A replica of a round tower in Dalkey granite, 168½ft tall, stands near the tomb of O'Connell; his crypt and the tower were both completed in 1869 to the design of George Petrie, and O'Connell ('the Liberator'), who died in 1847, was re-interred here. The tomb of Charles Stewart Parnell is crowned by an enormous granite rock. This is Ireland's largest cemetery, its oldest and most intriguing part being at the Prospect Square end, inside that disused gate. Here are the largest and most ornate headstones and crosses, including that of Sir Timothy O'Brien, Lord Mayor of Dublin, MP for the 'city of Cashel' and noted Patrick Street innkeeper and poteen distiller.

RATHFARNHAM CASTLE

Rathfarnham Road
The castle, whose grounds border the Castle golf course, has been occupied until recently by a community of Jesuits. A fine entrance gate was the casualty of road widening. The castle was built in the late 16th century by Archbishop Adam Loftus as an outpost to deter mountain men from attacking the city. It had a full garrison in 1641, when part of the city wall collapsed and rumours of a bid to seize Dublin Castle were afoot.

William Conolly, Speaker of the Irish House of Commons, bought the Rathfarnham fortress for £62,000 in 1724 from Philip, Duke of Wharton, who was in financial ruin through cards and drink. It later passed in turn to John Hoadly, Bellingham Boyle,

Nicholas Loftus and Lord Chancellor Blackburne. Over the years its Gothic windows were replaced and the Elizabethan battlements disappeared.

ROTUNDA HOSPITAL

Parnell Street and Square
This was the first maternity hospital in the British Isles to be built as such. It has had worldwide importance as a teaching centre since its inception. Its founder was Dr Bartholomew Mosse of Portlaoise (then Maryborough), who obtained a midwifery licence in 1742 from the Royal College of Physicians of Ireland, which encouraged medical men to involve themselves in maternity care while other royal colleges forbade their fellows to do so. Mosse opened his first maternity hospital in 1745 in the former Madame Violante's Theatre in George's Lane, Dublin, where Peg Woffington had performed, and engaged Richard Cassels in 1750 to design the new building in Parnell Street. Its biggest visual difference from Leinster House (see page 44), with which it shares a basic plan, is the three-storey tower with copper cupola. Mosse had intended to raise money by having an observatory in this tower. For the same reason, he turned the gardens into a pleasure

Richard Cassels designed the Rotunda Hospital for free in 1750, whereas Cramillion was paid 500 guineas for his beautiful baroque plasterwork in the chapel (top)

'vauxhall', laid out walks and charged admission. Hospital extensions cover these now. Cassels had intended to build the hospital across the top of what is now O'Connell Street, but the Gardiner property-owning family objected to this plan.

The hospital opened in 1757 as the Lying-in Hospital. The Rotunda, a lofty 80ft-diameter hall from which the hospital gets its present name, was designed in 1755 by George Ensor. It was fashionable in the 18th century as an Assembly Hall, and now houses a cinema. The 1895 Thomas Plunket Cairnes wing in Parnell Square West is named after a Drogheda brewer who donated generously to its building.

The Rotunda chapel, over the main entrance hall, is Dublin's most exquisite, with its high relief and beautifully-coloured plasterwork by Bartholomew Cramillion, completed in 1758.

Patrick Conway's old-style pub facing the hospital, well-known to expectant fathers, is older than the Rotunda, having opened in 1745.

There is fine walking to be enjoyed along the banks of the Royal Canal

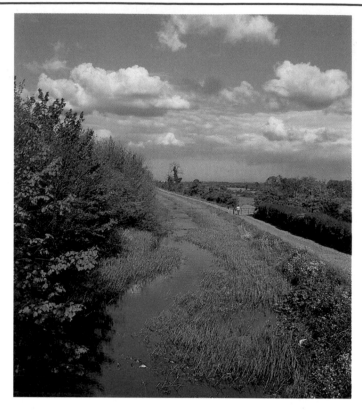

ROYAL CANAL

This waterway curves through the inner northside suburbs of Dublin just as the Grand Canal does on the south side. Its towpath may be walked for most of its urban length, from Newcomen Bridge at North Strand Road to the spreading suburb of Clonsilla, about seven miles and further if one likes. From Binns Bridge, in Drumcondra, with its rustic stile, the walk is very pleasant, becoming quite rural as it passes Cabra. Pleasure craft may be used on the water, and locks which had become ruinous have been repaired, entire new gates being made in some cases.

The Royal Canal Company was founded in 1789. Long John Binns, after whom bridges are named on both waterways, was a Grand Canal director who believed he had been insulted by fellow board members for being a shoemaker. He vowed to damage their business with a rival canal, and interested the Duke of Leinster in becoming a subscriber, on condition that the canal would pass Leinster's mansion, Carton House near Maynooth, which it does. But as the waterway, sometimes still referred to as the Shoemaker's Canal, duplicated the Grand in linking the Liffey and Shannon, it lost money from the start. Even its passenger services from Broadstone to Mullingar did not save it. In the 1840s, a railway company bought it to lay tracks on banks owned by the canal, and a rail line still hugs it from the Liffey to Mullingar. A large square pond with swans and waterfowl in a park at the top of Blessington Street is a converted filterbed from days when an arm of the canal provided drinking water.

ROYAL COLLEGE OF SURGEONS

St Stephen's Green
This handsome building dominates the green's west—and originally least fashionable—side. It was designed by William Murray and built on the site of an old cemetery in 1825–27. It is decorated with a balustrade and ten engaged Tuscan columns. In the tympanum are figures of Greek deities, including those of Medicine and Health. Murray's son, William G Murray, coincidentally designed the Royal College of Physicians in Kildare Street, which was finished in 1864. The surgeons moved to the Green

from a hall in Mercer Street, beside Mercer's Hospital, formerly a leper colony. The area between their old and new homes had been the Raparee Fields, a criminal haunt, and as this tradition was slow to die, they were initially plagued by body-snatchers anxious to sell corpses.

The college, now with a large modern extension in York Street, has a pleasant interior, rooms such as the Colles Room being named after former distinguished surgeons. The boardroom has fine plasterwork in its vaulted ceiling. It also has a dent in the copper finger panel of a door, legacy of a bullet fired through the window when the college was occupied by Constance Countess Markievicz during the 1916 Rising. As a colonel in the volunteers she was forced to withdraw there, and promptly asked where the scalpels were kept, so as to use them in hand-to-hand encounters.

ROYAL DUBLIN SOCIETY

Ballsbridge
The Society's sprawling showgrounds in Merrion Road, flanked on the city side by the Victorian Gothic Pembroke town hall, later a school, were opened in 1879 on a 15-acre site, but the present area is over 50 acres. The show-ground buildings have included the Society's head offices since 1922. They are by George Wilkinson and later architects, and the muted classical frontage on Merrion Road has festooned urns

and the heads of sheep, cattle and horses, surmounted by a figure of Plenty in the tympanum over the main entrance. These heads underline the Society's great agricultural tradition; it was founded on 25 June 1731 in the rooms of the Philosophical Society in Trinity College, to improve the condition of the country and raise the status of the agricultural population. Its first headquarters were in the old parliament house in College Green (see Bank of Ireland, page 32), then in Grafton Street and Hawkins Street in turn before it moved to Leinster House, where it remained until 1922. The Society was involved in the foundations of the National Museum, Library and Art Gallery, and it was Dr Walter Wade, Professor of Botany to the Society, who laid out the present National Botanic Gardens.

The best way to view the large showgrounds in Ballsbridge is to attend one of the Society's most famous shows, the Spring Show in May or Dublin Horse Show in August. The latter includes the international Aga Khan showjumping contest, and is accompanied by hunt balls and other social activities in the city. The May show concentrates on farming, with agricultural machinery and other animals than horses. Many other shows are held in these grounds—coin and philatelic fairs, motor and boat shows, holiday and home equipment exhibitions—as well as

People flock to the RDS for the Spring Show and the Dublin Horse Show

many concerts and lectures, and there are smaller agricultural shows, concerned only with bulls, for instance; but the two main annual events, with all their sideshows, bring the entire complex into play.

The RDS also owns an exceptionally fine members' library. Beyond the grounds is Thomas Prior House, built in 1881 in curious Victorian style. It is now an RDS premises but was originally a school for the daughters of deceased Freemasons.

ROYAL HOSPITAL

Kilmainham
Dublin's only monumental 17th-century building, this was built between 1680 and 1685 for about £24,000 to the design of William Robinson, Surveyor-General of Ireland. (Christopher Wren is often wrongly named as its designer.) The Duke of Ormonde had ordered its building, at the behest of Charles II, as a home for army pensioners. These, easily spotted in the neighbourhood by their uniforms, were called locally until this century 'Chelsea pensioners', despite their Dublin address and the fact that the hospital was older

The fine clock-tower of the Royal Hospital dates from 1701

than its Chelsea counterpart.

The chapel has a notable stucco ceiling and its excellent wood-carvings (by James Tabary) were once thought to be the work of Grinling Gibbons. The building, with a rather quaint clock-tower and four ranges around a quadrangle, has one of the finest interiors in Dublin. It was a police barrack for some time after its original occupation ended, but was extensively renovated by the Office of Public Works in the 1970s with a view to siting a folk section of the National Museum here. Many large items belonging to the museum were stored in the building while the restoration went on, but had to be removed again when the decision was taken to open the place as an 'EEC conference centre' instead.

The ornate Kilmainham gate has a pretentious side tower. Designed by Francis Johnston in 1812, this gate, then called Richmond Tower, spanned the road at Watling Street bridge, near Guinness's, before being removed in numbered stones and re-erected here. Just inside it are two cemeteries; the larger, Bully's Acre, Dublin's oldest, is said to contain the grave of Murrough, son of Brian Boru, and that of 1803 revolutionary Robert Emmet. Emmet was officially recorded as having been exhumed from here for reburial, but many disbelieve this. The whereabouts of his remains are a matter of continued controversy. The other cemetery contains graves of pensioners and some British soldiers killed in the 1916 Rising.

St Ann's, an 18th-century church to which a neo-Norman façade was added in 1869. 13th-century St Audoen's (inset) is Dublin's oldest parish church

ST ANDREW'S CHURCH

St Andrew's Street
Not to be confused with the Roman Catholic St Andrew's in Westland Row, this church was built (1860–73) to designs of Charles Lanyon on the site of the ancient nunnery of St Mary de Hogge. Its Gothic style, with dominant spire and exterior arcade, is somewhat cumbersome. A crowned pillar commemorates members of the Dublin company of Imperial Yeomanry killed in the Boer War. Across the road, behind the angle of the present Church Lane and Suffolk Street, the Viking 'thingmote' (ceremonial mound), 40ft high and 240ft in circumference, survived until 1661, being levelled to fill holes in what is now Nassau Street. Henry II met Irish chiefs here in 1172.

ST ANN'S CHURCH

Dawson Street
The church's imposing façade has a neo-Romanesque appearance. Built in pale granite, it is interspersed with single redbrick courses, a style typical of the work of Sir Thomas Deane and Benjamin Woodward, but far more strikingly exemplified in the church's parochial school and hall (1857–58) which stood around the corner in Molesworth Street until 1978. These were the subject of one of the most bitter clashes between preservationists and demolishers, the dispute lasting four years.

St Ann's, now noted for lunch-time recitals, is much older than its façade, and an unusual shelf to the left of the altar in its galleried interior fulfils the terms of a 1723 bequest. Lord Theophilus Newtown of Newtown Butler left £13 a year to the poor of St Ann's parish, to be distributed in the form of five shillings' worth of bread per week. The shelf was erected to hold the bread.

Beside the church is the Royal Irish Academy (No 19), with one of Ireland's finest libraries.

ST AUDOEN'S CHURCHES

High Street
Going up Bridge Street from the Liffey and turning left into Cook Street, a preserved stretch of city wall is reached, containing St Audoen's Arch, the last remaining city gate. Steps lead to the Norman west tower of the Protestant or 'old' St Audoen's. Only about a quarter of its area is now roofed. Some historians claim that the roofed part dates from about AD650, others say that the west doorway of 1169 is the church's oldest part. A pre-Norse church of St Columcille was on this site, and some of its structure may be incorporated in St Audoen's. The tower contains Ireland's three oldest bells, dating from 1423, and others from 1658 and 1694. Butchers, bakers, smiths and bricklayers once had guild chapels in the church.

The Roman Catholic St Audoen's abuts the other church and is reached from High Street, which was the main street of the walled city. It was designed by Patrick Byrne and opened in 1846, but the fine Corinthian portico dates from 1899. The church has traditional links with Dublin's Italian community and was sometimes visited by Giovanni Montini before he became Pope Paul VI. Its organ, an early Walker (London), is now a rarity.

ST CATHERINE'S CHURCH

Thomas Street
Used in recent times for exhibitions and concerts, St Catherine's was designed by John Smith and built between 1760 and 1769. It has a broad Tuscan façade and a square tower, and is a handsome but scarcely memorable building. It was completely restored by Dublin Corporation at the end of the 1970s and is an officially preserved building, given a new role as a museum. This church replaces one of the same name built in the 1180s by the monks of the abbey of St Thomas Becket.

On 20 September 1803 Robert Emmet was executed in the roadway opposite St Catherine's, after his insurrection, which included a plan to capture Dublin Castle, went disastrously wrong. A sign on the western part of the church railings indicates the spot.

Broad Bridgefoot Street faces the church; to the street's left was the Marshalsea of 1740, a debtors' prison which later became a notorious slum.

ST FRANCIS XAVIER CHURCH

Upper Gardiner Street
The church's most striking feature is the Italian high altarpiece, which is Dublin's finest. Its four 25ft Corinthian pillars look like green marble, but are built around timber cores by the Italian scagliola process, using powdered marble and paint. The altar is richly decorated with lapis lazuli. The church has a splendid coffered ceiling with high-relief rosettes, and the side chapels also repay attention. Designed by Joseph B Keane, this Jesuit church (1829–32) was originally intended for Great Charles Street, beyond Mountjoy Square. Its classical façade now stands at the very edge of the Gardiner family's great Georgian development. It is featured in Joyce's story *Grace*.

The convent beside the church has an extra storey over part of its length, added as a sanatorium during a devastating outbreak of cholera in 1832–34.

ST GEORGE'S CHURCH

Hardwicke Place, off Temple Street
St George's, completed in 1814, is possibly Francis Johnston's finest work. It has often been likened to London's St Martin-in-the-Fields, but this is only a general impression, and the differences are distinct. Standing on a street island, St George's is a Greek Ionic gem, with four fluted columns in the portico and a five-storey clocktower terminating in a slender spire, bringing the height to almost 200ft. Inside is Evie Hone stained glass. One is struck on entering the building by its great breadth; the roof span is 65ft.

The church's celebrated chime of bells was presented by the architect. Johnston was a keen campanologist and had built a four-storey belltower in his back garden at No 64 Eccles Street, but complaints from neighbours forced him to part with the bells. St George's received them with a stipulation that they be rung in his honour at certain times in perpetuity. Their sound is still a feature of the neighbourhood on Sunday and Wednesday nights, except at times of repair. In 1836, after their installation, engineers John and Robert Mallet inserted necessary iron arches in the roof to take the extra weight.

The municipal flats now facing the church follow the crescent line of the old Georgian layout, of which the church was the centrepiece, but 'George's Pocket', the cul-de-sac behind the apse, has not been preserved. Sir John Eccles's St George's (1714) is now only a castellated tower in a civic playground.

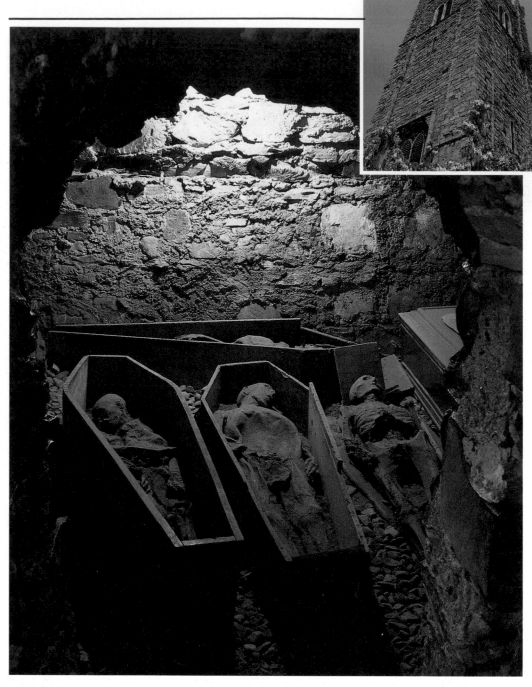

ST MARY'S CHURCH

Mary Street
The unobtrusive church is on a corner beyond Marks & Spencer as one approaches from O'Connell Street. It lies across the top of Wolfe Tone Park, its former burial ground. It became a parish church in 1697 and was soon Dublin's most fashionable. In it were baptised the Earl of Charlemont in 1728, Richard Brinsley Sheridan in 1751, Theobald Wolfe Tone in 1763, Sir William Rowan Hamilton, the renowned mathematician, in 1805 and playwright Sean O'Casey in 1880. Arthur Guinness and Ann Lee were married here in 1793. Dean Swift was a visitor to the church, and John Wesley preached here in 1747. Lord Norbury (a duellist

who became Chief Justice) is buried in what is now the park.

The church has a fine galleried interior and box pews, with carvings of early 18th-century figures on the organ case. The large ornate window in the east end has Baroque scroll adornments. The big Georgian doorway in the west front is a later addition.

ST MARY'S ABBEY

Meetinghouse Lane
Behind Capel Street and off a street named Mary's Abbey, the lane's warehouses hide the preserved 1180 chapter house of this 1156 abbey. The six-foot drop to its floor shows how levels have risen over the centuries. It is 45ft long and 24ft wide, and has a vaulted

roof with groin and crossribs. The mouldings of the ribs, very similar to those in the chapter house of Buildwas Abbey in Shropshire, establish the date of the building. It is rarely open to the general public, on-the-spot arrangements usually having to be made to view it.

The abbey was the largest pre-Reformation building on the north side of the Liffey. A Cistercian foundation, it had land stretching as far east as what is now Ballybough. Its cemetery now lies under parts of Green Street and North King Street. In this chapter house Lord 'Silken' Thomas Fitzgerald, acting as Lord Deputy and chairing a meeting of the Supreme Council in 1534, heard a false rumour that his father had been executed by Henry VIII. He flung his sword on the council

St Michan's 12th-century, 120ft-high tower. Some of its mummified bodies are indeed old, and guides would have you believe one was a Crusader

table and renounced his allegiance, starting a revolution which ended with his execution at Tyburn.

The Abbey was preceded on this site by a Benedictine monastery founded in 1038, or possibly a century earlier.

ST MARY'S PRO-CATHEDRAL

See Pro-Cathedral (page 54).

ST MICHAN'S CHURCH

Lower Church Street

A Danish church of 1095, almost totally rebuilt in 1686, this has a battlemented west tower and beautiful wood carving. Handel is believed to have played its organ (surviving) in 1742, the year of the first public performance of his *Messiah*, which took place across the Liffey in Fishamble Street.

Corpses lie in the church vaults in a state akin to natural mummification; this is due possibly to the very dry atmosphere caused by the magnesium lime from which the vaults are cut, and possibly to the presence of tannic acid, found in oak bark. The church stands on what was the edge of the great Oxmantown oak forest, which is said to have supplied William II with roof timbers for Westminster Hall in 1098.

ST PATRICK'S CATHEDRAL

Patrick Street

The Cathedral occupies the site of a Celtic Church of St Patrick, probably founded by that saint. The sacred associations of the place may explain the presence of such a large building on a marshy site. The River Poddle flows under the Cathedral, making a crypt impossible as water is less than eight feet below the floor. A holy well associated with the saint is now under the park adjoining the building. The first authentic record of the Cathedral's construction is dated 3 April 1225; the belief that it was begun in 1191 may be from older stones which formed a gate to an earlier timber church.

Henry de Londres, distrusting such monastic establishments as Christ Church, wanted a dean and chapter sympathetic to his views, so he raised St Patrick's (the older edifice) to cathedral status in 1213, as it was outside the city walls and Christ Church jurisdiction. Today it is the National Cathedral of the

Church of Ireland. The present lady chapel was completed in 1270. In 1316, after a storm had blown down the spire, the citizens, panicked by the proximity of Edward de Bruce, set the building on fire and art treasures were looted. After a more serious fire in 1362 Archbishop Thomas Minot built the tower which now supports the spire of 1749, bringing the cathedral's height to 230ft. The public clock in the tower is successor to one placed there by order of Elizabeth I.

The Interior

The stone roof and four graceful arches of the crossing have been repaired, but never altered. The original groining can be seen here and over parts of the choir, south transept and nave. Beside a Gothic door leading to the robing rooms is a marble bust of Jonathan Swift, Dean of St Patrick's for over 30 years, and over the door is Swift's

epitaph with that of Hester Johnson, Swift's 'Stella', on the door's other side. Swift and Stella are buried nearby in the nave. The Iveagh window in the north transept, by Frank Brangwyn, was erected in memory of the first Lord Iveagh by his children. The spiral staircase (1901) going to the organ chamber is modelled on one in Mainz Cathedral.

There are eight bays on each side of the nave, four in the choir and three in each transept. On the north side the three piers nearest the west end are seen to be higher and wider than the others, causing two arches to rise above the neighbouring string course. They are in Cheshire stone, not the original Somerset limestone; this infelicity dates from the 14th-century repairs.

The Cathedral can be seen from within to be a beautifully proportioned Latin cross.

Restoration

In 1864 Benjamin Lee Guinness financed a four-year restoration of St Patrick's, which included a new north transept, nave roof, middle storey of the nave, south wall in native granite and the addition of flying buttresses. The Guinness firm later laid out the Cathedral park on the site of former slums. It is said that in the service to mark the restoration the Dean began his sermon with the words: 'Today I take my text from Hebrews [he brews] XX.' (XX is a symbol used in grading stout.)

St Patrick's (below, and plaque on gate, left) was built originally near the site of the saint's Holy Well; it was completely restored in the mid-19th century

ST STEPHEN'S GREEN

St Stephen's Green is one of the biggest city squares in the world, and reputedly Europe's biggest. Its central area has been enclosed since 1663, when the west side was a place of execution. Outside the central area, opposite Dawson Street, is a fountain presented by Lady Laura Grattan in 1880. The entrance arch facing the top of Grafton Street is a memorial to members of the Royal Dublin Fusiliers killed in the Boer War, whose names are engraved in its underside. On the west side, a statue of Robert Emmet faces his birthplace at No 124 (demolished). A seated statue (1891) by Thomas Farrell shows Lord Ardilaun, the brewer who opened the green to the public in 1880 and laid it out as the beautiful park it is today. The statue, head slightly inclined, is looking precisely in the direction of St James's Gate brewery. Iron capstans on low granite posts at the kerbs of the green are a reminder that chains hung here when the general public was excluded.

On the south side a seat opposite Newman House is dedicated to James Joyce and his father. Joyce was a student in the Catholic University here. Just inside the gate at the south-east corner is a group of three bronze female figures over a fountain, the Three Fates spinning and measuring the thread of humanity's destiny, by Josef Wackerle. A walk along the east side ends at Edward Delaney's bronze statue of Wolfe Tone.

The Park
Entering opposite Grafton Street, the visitor sees a large rough stone with a likeness of Fenian leader O'Donovan-Rossa. Much of the northern half of the park is occupied by an artificial lake, with geese and ducks, crossed by a rustic bridge; on the promontory south of the lake is a 1967 W B Yeats memorial by Henry Moore. Near it are three bronze busts, one of the poet James Clarence Mangan with marble medallion of Roisin Dubh (Dark Rosaleen, a personification of Ireland); Mangan lived at No 6 York Street, off the green's west side. Another bust is of Constance Countess Markievicz, the first woman to be elected to the British House of Commons although she never took her seat. The third is of poet Tom Kettle, killed at the Battle of the Somme. A stone seat nearby commemorates Anna Maria Haslam (1829–1922) and Thomas Haslam (1825–1917), in

Memorials abound in delightful 22-acre St Stephen's Green: nationalist Robert Emmet (opposite top), poet James Mangan (left), while the Three Fates keep watch over man's destiny

recognition of their work for the enfranchisement of women.

A little eastward, a memorial to Louie Bennett (1870–1956), a founder of the Irish Women Workers' Union, takes the form of a small garden for the blind. Instead of flowers it has robust plants that can withstand handling, with metal labels in braille. Beyond the children's play area south of this is a memorial to members of Fianna Eireann.

The architecture around St Stephen's Green is extremely varied, with unusual embellishments like these 1730 railings outside Iveagh House

The Buildings

The green is encircled by magnificent 18th- and 19th-century buildings. The Shelbourne Hotel dates from 1867, replacing premises acquired in 1824. The Constitution of the Irish Free State was drafted in Room 112. Internal doors were deliberately made wide enough to accommodate ladies' bustles and the hotel is traditionally associated with leading social functions. On the way towards Grafton Street, No 22, with a fine roofed balcony, is the Friendly Brothers' House, No 17 is the University Club; and stone-fronted No 9, where Sir Walter Scott stayed, is the Stephen's Green Club. No 8 is a splendid building with a double sweep of steps.

The green's east side retains more Georgian character than the others. The Office of Public Works (No 51) with granite Egyptian-style pillars, is notable. Loreto Girls' College, Nos 53 and 54, is a celebrated academy.

See also Iveagh House, Royal College of Surgeons and University Church.

ST WERBURGH'S CHURCH

Werburgh Street

The lovely classical façade is part of a 1759 rebuilding; the church had been badly damaged by fire in 1754. There was a Church of St Martin of Tours on this spot before the Anglo-Norman invasion, shortly after which the first St Werburgh's was built. There was another rebuilding in 1662. The present fine interior gallery was designed by John Smith and built in 1767. There is a beautifully carved pulpit, possibly by Grinling Gibbons. A 160ft tower and spire were added the following year, giving the church considerable stature. The tower is seen in James Malton's celebrated print of Dublin Castle. It was demolished in 1810 because of official fears in the wake of Robert Emmet's uprising that it could be used for spying on the castle, or for ballistic attacks.

The vaults of St Werburgh's contain the remains of 1798 revolutionary Lord Edward Fitzgerald, who died in the now-demolished Newgate Prison in Halston Street. The porch contains ancient fire-fighting equipment, dating from days when parish churches were mustering points for voluntary firemen.

A short distance above the church on the same side of the street an employment exchange stands on the site of Jonathan Swift's 1667 birthplace, Hoey's Court.

There is a side entrance to St Werburgh's through No 8 Bristol Buildings.

TAILORS' HALL

Back Lane

Despite the unpromising sound of the address, which is behind the south side of High Street facing the churches, this was one of the most prestigious guildhalls in the city. It was unusual for such halls to boast a courtyard. Tailors' Hall, built in 1706–7, added its courtyard seven years later. Most of the weavers who supplied the tailors were based a little to the south of the hall at that time.

The hall's restoration is recent and was inspired by fears that this oldest surviving city guildhall would become a dangerous ruin and be arbitrarily demolished. This had happened to the Weavers' Hall in the Coombe. There has also been widespread demolition of Queen Anne buildings, this hall being the last one of any significance in its area. A fund was established to save it, and it was re-opened as a place for functions. It is now the home of An Taisce, the Irish National Trust.

In the room where the guild formerly met are long, beautifully proportioned Queen Anne windows and the dark timber committee rostrum with its serrated pediment, restored after a search for missing pieces. The building retains the original 'sugar barley twist' Jacobean-style banisters.

List of Masters in Tailors' Hall. From 1792, when the General Catholic Committee met here, it was known as the Back Lane Parliament

The 300ft frontage of Queen Elizabeth's 'College of the Holy and Undivided Trinity'. In the beautiful Long Room of the Old Library (right) stand busts of famous Trinity alumni

TRINITY COLLEGE

College Green
Trinity College was founded in 1592 under a charter of Elizabeth I 'for the planting of learning, the increasing of civility and the establishing of true religion within the realm'. The religion referred to was Protestantism, and for many years Trinity was seen in the rest of the country as the mainspring of Puritan Dublin thought. It is correctly called Dublin University, Trinity being its sole college. The first students arrived in 1594.

Statues of Edmund Burke and Oliver Goldsmith by John H Foley stand in front of Trinity in College Green. They were 18th-century college contemporaries, but did not become friends until later life. The long Palladian west front behind them (1752–60) is attributed to Henry Keane and John Sanderson, but may have been the work of Theodore Jacobsen, amateur architect of the London Foundling Hospital. The vestibule leads to Front Square, with lawns, and cobbled Parliament Square, whose joint area was the site of the 1166 Augustinian Priory of All Hallows, founded by Dermot MacMurrough, King of Leinster. Its steeple was a landmark to navigators, and is symbolically replaced by the TCD campanile (1852) by Charles Lanyon, near the centre of Library Square. A five-storey belltower by Richard Cassels preceded the campanile.

The Corinthian porticoes of the chapel (left) and examination hall face each other across the near side of Parliament Square, and are the limits of the formal classicism in the Trinity layout. Both are by William Chambers and have barrel-vaulted ceilings and plasterwork by Michael Stapleton, but they are not quite identical. The examination

hall, originally a public theatre, was completed about 1785. Work on the chapel went on from 1787 to 1800.

Beyond the chapel and set back from it is the dining hall, whose façade, with clock, looks like a smaller version of the college's west front. It was designed by Hugh Darley in 1758 to replace a dining hall erected by Richard Cassels, which had been condemned after several masonry falls. A great fireplace surround in black Kilkenny marble, which Cassels had had carved by David Sheehan for the old hall, is in the common room, over the entrance. Facing the hall across Parliament Square is the science and music reading room (1937).

The Library
Beyond the campanile, Library Square has shaven lawns, antique lamps and old Oregon maples with wired up branches. On its left is the long grey Elizabethan-style Graduates' Memorial Building by Sir Thomas Drew, completed in 1900, behind which is an area called 'Botany Bay', with tennis courts and students' apartments. On the square's right is the huge block of Thomas Burgh's 1712 Library, which was altered considerably in 1860 by Deane and Woodward.

The Library (with sculpture), started by subscriptions from Elizabeth's army

The Long Room, which is 210ft long and 41ft broad, was 40ft high even before they raised it significantly and gave it a barrel-vaulted ceiling, which explains the high pitch of the building's roof. What had been already the largest library reading room in Europe thus became immense.

Book of Kells
The Library's chief treasure, the *Book of Kells* is normally kept in this room. A Latin text of the four Gospels with magnificent and intricate illuminated pages, it dates from about AD800. Originally a single volume, it was repaired in

1953 and re-bound in four volumes, two of which are usually on display, one open at an illuminated page and one showing text. The openings change regularly. Other precious manuscripts include the *Book of Durrow* and *Book of Armagh*, of the 7th and 9th centuries. On display is Elizabeth I's coat of arms which is believed to have hung over the college entrance, and the medieval O'Neill harp, popularly called Brian Boru's harp and used as the Guinness trademark. The room houses about 200,000 of Trinity's oldest books; the entire stock of over 2,500,000 volumes occupies shelving lengthening by about half-a-mile a year. Since the 1801 Copyright Act the college has the right to claim a copy of every British or Irish publication.

The Library is open on weekdays and Saturday mornings.

Museum
Behind the Library is Fellows' Square with the modern arts block and Douglas Hyde gallery beyond it. The eastern end of Library Square is closed by the red-brick Queen Anne apartments called the Rubrics (begun in 1700), the oldest existing part of the college and partly financed by Queen Anne's grant of £3,000, which she raised by increasing tobacco duty. In New Square are the bookshop and Berkeley Library (1967), built to

Paul Koralek's prize-winning design. Beyond that is Deane and Woodward's Museum building (1854), a lovely edifice of strong Ruskinian influence, adorned with marble medallions copied from the ducal palace in Venice. Its interior is decidedly Moorish.

East of New Square is the rugby ground, with College Park south of it. A cricket ball struck from here by W G Grace once broke a window in the Kildare Street Club. A suggestion to build the Wellington Monument here was considered in 1814. In 1775 Provost Hely Hutchinson banned public access to the park on the grounds that it had become a 'public walk for company of the lowest and worst kind', obviously unfit for students who were allowed to play cards on Sundays only.

Back on the north side of New Square is a temple-like printing house by Richard Cassels, built 1734–36. In 1738 this produced the first book totally in Greek to be printed in Ireland, an edition of Plato's *Dialogues*.

Outside the college, the Provost's house at the foot of Grafton Street was built in 1759. Its façade design is Palladian, and was used for a London house of one General Wade and a house in Potsdam for Frederick the Great. The Dublin example is sole survivor of the trio.

The striking white marble Pieta on the lawn of Tyrone House was a post-war gift to the people of Ireland from the Italian nation

TYRONE HOUSE

Marlborough Street
Now part of the Department of Education, the square granite house to the right of the railed open space facing the Pro-Cathedral was designed by Richard Cassels and built mostly in 1740 for Sir Marcus Beresford, Earl of Tyrone. With three storeys over a rough stone basement, its sombre aspect is scarcely relieved by the six square pillars in its portico. It originally had a Venetian window above the portico, and it still boasts Francini plasterwork and a fine rear staircase. A similar building, in size and scale but not in detail, stands at the other side of the open space, but this is a 19th-century construction.

In the grounds is a white marble *Pieta* on a lawn. This is a 1930 work by Ermenegildo Luppi of Rome, and was presented to Ireland by the Italian Government in 1948 in gratitude for post-war Irish aid to Italy. The cost of transporting it to Ireland was borne by the Italian community of Dublin.

Nearby Waterford Street was formerly Tyrone Street, after the Earl, the name being changed because of former 'red light' associations.

The Book of Kells, *taken from the Monastery of Kells to TCD by Cromwell's troops*

UNIVERSITY CHURCH

St Stephen's Green

Beside Newman House, to which it is linked by a 'floating' canopy over a red-brick entrance which gives no hint of the interior, the church was commissioned by Cardinal Newman as part of his Catholic University. He brought John Hungerford Pollen from England to design it as a collegiate church and it was built between 1854 and 1856. A neo-Byzantine style was chosen, and the architect was heavily influenced by Newman himself. The interior is polychromatic; the canopied altar is set in a deeply curved and highly decorated apse, with an arcaded choir on the left.

The design gave rise to controversy, purists asserting that it was comically unsuitable for Dublin and typified Newman's aloof and humourless character. But it has been generally admitted that the church has points of real beauty and is extraordinarily faithful to the atmosphere of its Byzantine prototypes.

Since the removal of the nucleus of University College Dublin to suburban Belfield, the church has fulfilled a different role and has long been recognised as the most fashionable place for Catholic weddings.

The interior of University Church displays the beauty of Irish marble. University College originated in the Catholic University of Ireland founded in 1854 by Cardinal Newman. Above is its Engineering School

UNIVERSITY COLLEGE DUBLIN

Earlsfort Terrace and Belfield

A constituent college of the National University, UCD accommodates most of its faculties, including arts, commerce and physics, in a modern campus at Belfield, on Stillorgan Road, where the sports grounds, including an excellent running track, are also located in a spacious and pleasant complex.

Some departments are still housed in the older buildings at Earlsfort Terrace. The main block (1914–19) with long limestone façade and Ionic pillars, was designed by R M Butler. Its erection followed an Act of 1908 which made the Catholic university in St Stephen's Green and the Queen's colleges in Cork and Galway parts of a new national university. Earlsfort Terrace was chosen partly because of its nearness to the Green (see Newman House, under Iveagh House, page 43), partly because an older examining body, the Royal University of Ireland, had occupied buildings there. Earlsfort Terrace's main public interest now is in the fact that part of it has been converted into the splendid National Concert Hall, whose spacious central stage is used for televised functions and fashion shows as well as for performances of music.

CITY WALKS

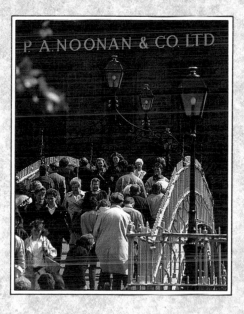

*Crossing the Halfpenny Bridge (see the River Walk, page
71) named after the toll once charged for crossing. Virtually
a symbol of Dublin, it arches gracefully over the Liffey*

South to North

This walk across the very heart of the city, from St Stephen's Green to Parnell Square, takes in Dublin's main shopping streets: Grafton Street, originally a country lane and now chic and expensive; West-moreland Street, which was laid out as a shopping street in 1800; and long, spacious O'Connell Street, planned on a grand scale in 1784 and now alive with ice-cream parlours and big stores. The surrounding side streets and arcades abound in antiques, lace and Celtic crafts.

A period piece in St Stephen's Green

Allow: 1¼ hours

Start at the Shelbourne Hotel, St Stephen's Green.

1 SHELBOURNE HOTEL

The hotel was founded in 1824 but the present Victorian building dates only from 1867. The four bronze female figures represent a pair of Nubian princesses and their slave girls (observe the latters' fettered ankles). Across the road at the corner of the Park is the statue of the Irish Patriot Wolfe Tone.

Cross the road and enter St Stephen's Green Park at the entrance behind Wolfe Tone's statue and take the path due south along the railings. Leave the park at the Three Fates Fountain, a gift from the German people in recognition of Ireland's help in relieving distress in Germany after the last war. Walk along the pavement beside the railings, stopping opposite Iveagh House.

Iveagh House retains its ornate street lamps and railings

2 IVEAGH HOUSE

Iveagh House is the headquarters of the Department of Foreign Affairs. The building was constructed in 1736 and in 1939 was presented by the Guinness family to the Irish nation. Its interior is one of the richest in Dublin. A little further down the street is Newman House and University Church, the site of Dublin's first Catholic University.

Enter the park again and walk in the direction of the bandstand, cross the central intersection between the fountains and stroll over the rustic bridge, turning left along the duck pond towards Fusiliers' Arch.

3 FUSILIERS' ARCH

Also known as Traitors' Arch, this memorial was built to commemorate the members of the Royal Dublin Fusiliers who lost their lives in the Boer War of 1899–1900. Their names are inscribed in the panels under the arch. The world-famous Royal College of Surgeons is to the left of the arch on the west side of St Stephen's Green.

Head down Grafton Street, a premier pedestrianised shopping precinct which is reawakening to an appreciation of its Victorian heritage. Halfway down the left-hand side is Johnston's Court, an

Walk up O'Connell Street along the central pavement. From here you can best observe both sides of Dublin's principal thoroughfare which had to be almost rebuilt after the destruction of 1916 and the Civil War of 1922. The pride of the street is the General Post Office.

6 GENERAL POST OFFICE
Built in 1815 (architect Francis Johnston) this building is revered as the birthplace of the modern Irish state. On Easter Monday 1916 Patrick Pearse read the proclamation of the Irish Republic from the main door and the bloody rising which followed, although suppressed in one week, led to Independence six years later.

The pedestrian street which runs down the right side of the GPO is Henry Street, Dublin's busiest — with 145,000 pedestrians daily — and most popular shopping street

At the end of O'Connell Street, at the intersection with Parnell Street, is the striking monument to Charles Stewart Parnell, a leading Irish Nationalist in the 1880s. Turn left here, and then right into Parnell Square West, to arrive at the Rotunda Hospital.

7 ROTUNDA HOSPITAL
Designed by Richard Cassels and opened in 1757, this institution was the first maternity hospital in the British Isles. The hospital gets its name from the round building now housing the Ambassador Cinema. Its chapel, Dublin's best example of baroque decoration, is open.

Walk up Cavendish Row. The disused drinking fountain is another example of the city's rich collection of street furniture. Next is the Gate Theatre which was founded in 1928 and has since played an important role in establishing Dublin's theatrical reputation. Enter the Garden of Remembrance at the top of Parnell Square.

Garden of Remembrance—symbolic railings

attractive narrow passageway leading to a number of interesting shopping complexes. At the bottom of Grafton Street keep going past Trinity College and the Bank of Ireland, and walk down Westmoreland Street until you reach O'Connell Bridge.

4 O'CONNELL BRIDGE
This handsome bridge has the distinction of measuring more in its width than its length. The building of the first bridge here in 1797 — originally Carlisle Bridge — changed the whole axis of the city, transforming quiet residential areas into streets throbbing with commercialism. The lamps on the bridge were once lit by gas.
Ahead is the O'Connell Monument.

Statues line O'Connell Street: Jim Larkin was a great trade union leader

5 O'CONNELL MONUMENT
Daniel O'Connell, known as the Liberator, won Catholic emancipation in 1829. This group of statuary was executed by the eminent Irish sculptor John Henry Foley and erected in 1854. If you look closely you will see several bullet holes in the winged Victories: they are souvenirs from the Easter Rising of 1916.

Other statues along the street include the over large bronze of James Larkin who, against fierce opposition, founded the trade union movement in Ireland.

8 GARDEN OF REMEMBRANCE
Opened in 1966 to commemorate all those who died for Irish Freedom, this small park is a quiet oasis from the busy streets. The large sculpture is by Oisin Kelly and represents the Children of Lir being transformed into swans. Over the railings can be seen the Municipal Gallery of Modern Art.
The walk ends here.

The River Walk

A *fascinating tour criss-crossing the River Liffey and the warren of narrow side streets to see the heritage left behind from the arrival of the Vikings in* AD841 *to the present day.*

Allow: 1½ hours

Start the walk from the Steyne Stone, a monument at the junction of College Green and D'Olier Street and head up Hawkins Street towards the river.

1 THE STEYNE STONE

The River Liffey once covered this area and it was here that the Vikings commemorated their landing by erecting a 13ft-high stone slab. The original stone disappeared after the new quay wall pushed back the river in the 17th century.

Turn right at the Sheahan Memorial (which honours a Dublin Metropolitan policeman who gave his life in 1905 trying to save others overcome by sewer gas) and proceed down Burgh Quay and George's Quay.

Hope and her anchor crown the dome of the Custom House, which dominates the Liffey to the east (above)

2 CUSTOM HOUSE

Across the river is Dublin's finest public building, the recently-restored Custom House. The neighbouring Custom House Dock is now the scene of the country's biggest ever renewal project, which will see the transformation of warehouses into a quality development featuring a conference centre, hotel, leisure complexes, museums, housing precincts, shops and light industry.

Cross Talbot Memorial Bridge and walk around the back of the Custom House (through the gardens if open) to view the memorial and fountain representing Ireland comforting one of her fallen sons. Continue around to Butt Bridge and turn right up Eden Quay, past O'Connell Bridge and along Batchelors Walk until you reach the Halfpenny Bridge.

3 HALFPENNY BRIDGE

This elegant metal bridge, now almost the symbol of Dublin, was built as Wellington Bridge in 1816 when a toll of a halfpenny was charged to cross it.

Cross over the bridge — mind your hat if it is a breezy day — and walk under Merchant's Arch into what is developing as Dublin's equivalent of the Left Bank. Proceed along the narrow winding streets of eating places, craft shops, little theatres and pubs, taking the direction of Crown Alley, Cope Street, Cecilia Street, Temple Bar and Essex Street. Turn right when you reach Parliament Street and walk down to Grattan Bridge and the Sunlight Chambers.

Early advertising, in colour

4 SUNLIGHT CHAMBERS

A remarkable little turn-of-the-century building built by Lever Bros. The friezes around the exterior illustrate the labours of men, the merchandising of the raw materials for soap and the everyday use of soap. Their purpose, in an age before modern media advertising, was to promote the use of soap.

Continue along Essex Quay and turn up Fishamble Street.

5 FISHAMBLE STREET

This curving road was once the fish market ('fish shamble') of medieval Dublin. In 1742 Handel's *Messiah* had its first performance in Neil's Music Hall — now the iron works of Kennan & Sons.

Turn back to the Quays and walk past the new Civic Offices (the site of Europe's largest and most fruitful Viking excavations) noticing Christ Church in the background. Turn up Winetavern Street and take the next right into Cook Street to see a large remnant of the medieval city walls at St Audoen's Arch.

6 ST AUDOEN'S ARCH

This was one of the main gates in Dublin's extensive ring of ramparts and this section of wall dates from 1240. It is worth climbing the steps to the top to view and appreciate the restoration carried out by Dublin Corporation to mark European Architectural Heritage Year in 1975.

Climb down the flight of steps at the far end of the park and head down Bridge Street towards the Liffey again. On the left is Dublin's oldest pub, The Brazen Head.

7 THE BRAZEN HEAD

The present building dates from 1668 but the establishment is thought to go back to 1198. Various insurrections (all unsuccessful) were planned here and the interior still reflects a cosy furtiveness. Traditional music is a feature, especially at weekends.

Before crossing the bridge take in the elegance, across the river, of the Four Courts, complementary to the Custom House further down the river. Walk the short distance up Church Street to St Michan's Church.

8 ST MICHAN'S

This is an historic church in its own right, first founded in 1095. But perhaps it is most famous for its crypt which contains several disintegrated coffins revealing the skeletons of their denizens whose skin is still preserved by the quality of the underground atmosphere. Some of the remains are certainly several hundred years old, and the guide may have you believe that one of them was a Crusader.

Return to the Quays and take any bus — or a 15-minute walk — back to the Centre.

Apt wood carvings in St Michan's: Handel played its Harris organ

The Phoenix Park

*S*ituated only 1¼ miles from O'Connell Street, the 1752 acres of the Phoenix Park contain a wealth of rolling grasslands, expansive city panoramas, shaded woods, curious monuments and noteworthy buildings. This itinerary will cover about an eighth of the entire park so if you like and you feel energetic enough, you can extend the suggested tour with a longer exploration.

Allow: 1½ hours.

The huge Wellington Monument (right) is by Sir Robert Smirke; nearby is the grim, deserted Magazine Fort which took 65 years to complete

Begin at the Parkgate Street entrance (buses 23, 25, 26, 51, 66, 67, 68, 69 or a 30-minute walk from O'Connell Street — a walk which will take you past Collin's Barracks, the oldest continuously-occupied barracks in the world). The road stretching straight ahead for over 2½ miles is named after Lord Chesterfield, the Lord Lieutenant who opened the Park for public use in 1745. Note the old-fashioned street lamps, still lit by gas, and the decorative cast-iron bench seats. Turn left across the field to The Wellington Monument.

1 WELLINGTON MONUMENT

This testimonial to the Duke of Wellington (who was born in Dublin) is 220ft high and was built between 1813 and 1861. Battle scenes depicted around the pedestal were cast from captured cannon.

Walk towards the road which will take you downhill towards the Magazine Fort. Note some interesting panoramas of the city to your left as you go.

2 MAGAZINE FORT

Built on Thomas' Hill and the former site of Phoenix House after which the Park is named, the fort dates from around 1738 and was used as a munitions store until the mid-20th century.

Circle the perimeter of the fort and come down to the road which leads up through the Khyber Valley. Take this route and from here on you may encounter some of the Park's animal inhabitants.

3 FLORA AND FAUNA

The calcareous grasslands support a rare native orchid and a violet. The main species of tree include oak, ash, beech, larch, cedar and cypress. Various hawthorn plantations are widespread. A herd of 300 fallow deer roams between Oxmantown Wood and the Fifteen Acres. Mammals also include foxes, badgers, stoats, hares, rabbits and squirrels. Birds are represented by blackbirds, thrushes, wrens, robins, tits, finches, magpies, jackdaws, rooks and jays. Larger varieties include pheasants, wood pigeons, kestrels, sparrowhawks and owls. Waterfowl include mallard, coots, waterhens and swans.

After walking for 10 minutes or so the towering Papal Cross will come into view. Make your way over to it.

4 PAPAL CROSS

The Cross was erected near the edge of the Fifteen Acres for the Papal visit to Ireland in 1979 when a staggering 1,200,000 people gathered here for the celebrations. Even now this is one of the most visited areas of the Park. The Residence of the Ambassador of the United States of America is visible through the trees behind the Cross.

Moving away from the Papal Cross head towards the main road passing the entrance to the Ambassador's Residence.

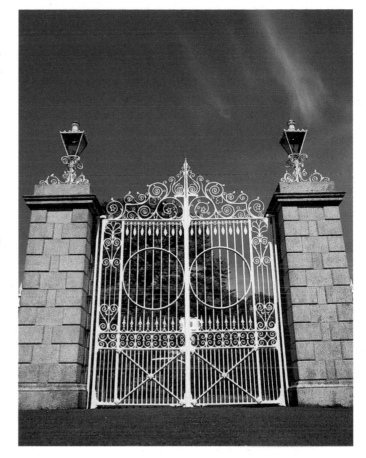

5 AMERICAN AMBASSADOR'S RESIDENCE

Built in 1776, it became the residence of the British Chief Secretary in 1782. This late-Georgian mansion was taken over as the residence of the US Ambassador in 1927. A quaint natural stone bridge is visible from the gate.

Cross the main road by the Phoenix

A view, across its lake, of the carefully planned Dublin zoo

Monument and proceed down towards Áras an Uachtaráin (House of the President).

6 ÁRAS AN UACHTARAIN

Through a deliberate gap in the screen of trees you can see the central portion of the building erected in 1751 which was later used as the Viceregal Lodge until Independence in 1922. It was then occupied by the Governor General and since 1937 has been the residence of the President of Ireland.

The gardens behind the gates of Áras an Uachtaráin were laid out in 1840 by the celebrated Decimus Burton

Continuing along the path or grass take the next left to bring you around past the Polo Grounds, past part of the Zoo (you can peep through the gaps in the screening) until you reach the back road. Turn right and walk past McKee Barracks and the Garda Headquarters.

7 GARDA HEADQUARTERS

Built in 1839–42 for the Royal Irish Constabulary, this building is now the HQ of the Irish Police Force and contains a Police Museum.

Turn right at the first junction and enter the 'Hollow' opposite the Zoo.

8 ZOOLOGICAL GARDENS

Opened in 1831 it is one of the oldest zoos in Europe. The MGM lion was bred here. Note the thatched entrance.

The Hollow is a natural amphitheatre and the Victorian bandstand is still used. From the Hollow enter the People's Garden, go down to the lake, up the steps at the end and walk past Army Headquarters which can be seen through the trees.

9 ARMY HEADQUARTERS

It started life as The Royal Infirmary in 1788 and was British Army Headquarters at the beginning of this century. It now houses the offices of the Department of Defence.

Now make your way back out of the Park and walk or take any bus back to the City Centre.

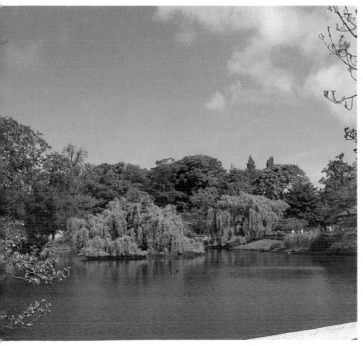

Georgian Streetscapes

*A*lthough it has to share space with fine Victorian neighbours and some modern developments, the splendour of 18th-century Georgian Dublin remains relatively intact around this section of the city.

Allow: 1¼ hours

The tour begins outside the gates of Trinity College. Pause for a few moments to view College Green.

1 COLLEGE GREEN
This was once the Commons of the medieval city where animals were grazed and the population was entertained by pageants. Trinity College arrived in 1592 and the colonnaded House of Parliament (now the Bank of Ireland) was begun in 1728. In the centre of College Green, with outstretched arm, is Henry Grattan, leader of the parliamentary opposition and an opponent of union with England. At the opposite corner is Fox's Tobacconists — reputed to have been the only shop in Northern Europe where you could still buy a Havana cigar during World War II.

Walk into Nassau Street and turn right into Dawson Street.

2 DAWSON STREET
A street of boutiques, travel agencies, airline offices and insurance companies. Halfway up is St Ann's Church (religious or cultural events take place daily at lunchtime); next door is the Royal Irish Academy (founded in 1785 to promote the study of Irish history and antiquities) and its neighbour is the 'Victorianised' Georgian house of Dublin's Lord Mayor, the Mansion House. Facing the top of the street from the opposite side of St Stephen's Green is a decorative horse-drinking fountain, a reminder of more leisurely days.

Turn left into St Stephen's Green and before you turn left again into Kildare Street you will notice the majestic Shelbourne Hotel, Dublin's premier hotel since 1824.

3 KILDARE STREET
This street boasts a fine collection of public buildings. Behind its magnificent iron gates lies Leinster House (1745), one time residence of the Earl of Kildare and now the seat of Dail Eireann (the Irish Parliament). On either side are the splendid buildings housing the National Library and the National Museum. Further down the same side is what was once the exclusive Kildare Street Club; the building is now shared by the Genealogical Office (where Irish family histories can be traced for you) and the French Cultural Centre.

Turn right up South Leinster Street and into Clare Street past the old open air bookstalls of the venerable Greene's Bookshop until you arrive at Merrion Square.

Leinster House, first of the great Georgian mansions built south of the Liffey

The observant visitor can spot many decorative details while walking round 18th-century Merrion Square

4 MERRION SQUARE
This is probably the best-preserved of the Georgian squares. Across the road at the corner with Lower Merrion Street is No 1 Merrion Square, home of Oscar Wilde when he was a child. Walking up Merrion Square West you will first see the National Gallery of Ireland and next to it the reverse façade of Leinster House. Flanking the other side of Leinster House is the Natural History Museum and in front of it is a statue of Surgeon Major T H Parke, an Irish explorer and doctor who was associated with many expeditions to Africa including those with H M Stanley, and the belated rescue attempt of Gordon in Khartoum. The impressive block of buildings in Upper Merrion Street is Government Buildings, headquarters of the principal government departments. Directly across the road, No 24 is the birthplace of Arthur Wellesley, 1st Duke of Wellington.

Proceed up Merrion Square South and appreciate the long unbroken view all the way up to St Stephen's Church, known affectionately to Dubliners as the 'Pepper-canister'. Divert for a while into the pleasant park and view the houses from a different perspective. Continue up to and around the back of the church, noting the name plaques on the houses and the Georgian doorways, each one different from its neighbour. You now see the Huband Bridge and the Grand Canal.

The Grand Canal basin—the 18th-century canal connects Dublin Bay with the Shannon, curving through the city's southern suburbs to a harbour near the Liffey's mouth

5 GRAND CANAL

Dublin has two canals, the Grand (south city) and the Royal (north city). The description 'inner city' is usually taken to mean the area between the canals. The canals were unused for years but a management plan has been prepared to restore them to a water and linear park.

Walk along the tow-path to Herbert Place and at Baggot Street Bridge turn right and head down Baggot Street. The modern headquarters of the Irish Tourist Board (Bord Failte), the Peat Board (Bord na Mona) *and Ireland's largest bank group, Bank of Ireland, are situated along this street.*

6 BAGGOT STREET

Notice the later-styled Georgian houses and the converted mews (where laneways intersect), and get occasional glimpses of the interesting rear views of the grand old town mansions.

Continue past the pubs of Baggot Street and Merrion Row to return to the Shelbourne Hotel.

The Liberties

These were the areas outside the medieval City Walls which were exempt from local jurisdiction and subject directly to the representatives of the King and the Pope. It was a very cosmopolitan part of Dublin when French, Dutch and Flemish Protestants arrived here in the 17th century to escape religious persecution in their homelands. Due to harsh trading restrictions, the industries they established collapsed in the next century and the area to this day has never fully recovered from the appalling poverty which ensued.

Allow: 1¼ hours

This tour starts at Cornmarket (buses 21A, 78A, 78B, or less than 15 minutes walk from Trinity College). Proceed up Francis Street to the Iveagh Market.

1 THE IVEAGH MARKET

This old clothes market was built by the munificent Earl of Iveagh (of the Guinness family) in 1907 to house displaced street vendors. Here real Dublin characters sell their wares with wit, shrewdness and a charming style peculiar to themselves. On the outside wall around the corner from the entrance is an extraordinary stone winking face — said to be Lord Iveagh himself.

Continue down Francis Street past numerous curio and antique shops until you reach a street simply called The Coombe. Pass a building with the curious title inscribed on the outside 'Widows House of the Parish of St Nicholas Without and St Luke'. This charity is now defunct. A short distance further up is the preserved gateway of the demolished and relocated Coombe Maternity Hospital.

Stone head at Iveagh Market, said to be that of Lord Iveagh himself

2 COOMBE HOSPITAL MEMORIAL

The history of the old hospital can be read from the plaque on the front of the gateway. Around the back the apt and imaginative names of fondly-remembered Dublin street characters are carved into the steps. Well worth a read.

Turn right into Meath Street, a busy thoroughfare of small shops, pubs and

markets, past St Catherine's Church (Catholic) until you reach Thomas Street. Keep your ear open for the rich local accents and turn of phrase.

3 THOMAS STREET

Thomas Street was laid down around 1180 and was once the retail heart of the Liberties that could satisfy all the requirements of the locals; but its position is less important today. On the right is the striking spire of St John and St Augustine — colloquially called John's Lane — an Augustinian foundation. The church was designed by Pugin. Nearer to where you are standing is the National College of Art and Design which functions in a converted distillery.

Now turn left up Thomas Street until you come to St Catherine's Church (formerly Church of Ireland, now a community centre).

4 ST CATHERINE'S CHURCH

St Catherine's was originally founded around 1180 by the monks of St Thomas' Abbey and the present building dates from 1765. Robert Emmet was hanged outside the Church after his abortive insurrection in 1803.

Keep going straight on into James's Street which is dominated on both sides by the Guinness Brewery.

5 GUINNESS BREWERY

As you pass Crane Street you can turn up to the converted Hop Store, now an exhibition centre. Back on James's Street the main entrance to the Brewery is through James's Gate over which the current year

Apart from the secondhand clothes stalls of Iveagh Market, Francis Street has a large number of antique and curio shops

James's Gate, the entrance to the Guinness Brewery

7 ROYAL HOSPITAL

This masterpiece was built between 1680 and 1684 and is French in character. It was designed as a Hospital for wounded and retired soldiers and as such preceded Chelsea. It was thoroughly restored in 1984 and is now a multi-purpose building containing exhibition, museum and function space.

Return to St John's Road and take any bus heading from Heuston Station to the city centre.

The Royal Hospital, Kilmainham

and the date of origin, 1759, are both painted. Take a short side trip up Echlin Street behind St James's Church to see the rear elevations of Guinness and discover the magnificence of Victorian industrial architecture.

After the brewery turn right into Steevens Lane. On the left is St Patrick's Hospital founded 'for the reception of aged lunaticks' from money left in the will of Jonathan Swift. Further down the road is Dr Steeven's Hospital founded in 1733 in a district remote from the city in order to prevent the spread of infections and plagues. Heuston Railway Station stands opposite the junction with St John's Road.

6 HEUSTON RAILWAY STATION

Constructed in 1844, Kingsbridge Station (as it was then known) was a monumental showpiece for the Great Southern and Western Railway Company. It is arguably one of the finest stations in these islands. The Victorian aspect of the platforms has also been retained.

Proceed up St John's Road and turn left for The Royal Hospital.

Commerce, Castle and Cathedrals

A tour around Viking and medieval Dublin.

Allow: 1½ hours

Start at St Andrew's Church in St Andrew's Street.

1 ST ANDREW'S CHURCH

Built in 1866 to replace an earlier church, it occupies the site of the Thingmote. This was a Viking assembly point for civic, judicial and military decision-making. The column in the churchyard remembers the Boer War.

Continue up South William Street passing the former Powerscourt House, now an imaginative shopping and craft centre complex. Next to it is the Dublin Civic Museum. This street is mainly populated by clothing manufacturers. Ahead is the old Mercer's Hospital founded on the site of the medieval St Stephen's Leper Hospital.

Turn right into Lower Stephen Street and cross the junction with Aungier Street into Upper Stephen Street. Note a plaque to Dunlop's first tyre factory. On the right, down Great Ship Street, are the disused Ship Street Barracks from which troops once protected the British Administration in Dublin Castle. Proceed past the new Corporation housing and turn left into Bride Street. Pass Peter Street where every Sunday morning one of the world's oldest bird markets takes place. Cross the road and turn right into Kevin Street.

2 KEVIN STREET

Kevin Street Garda Station was formerly the medieval Archbishops' Palace of St Sepulchre. The present gateposts, a coat-of-arms, a window,

Huguenot tombstones at the Cabbage Garden, off Kevin Street

an internal door and the thick walls remain from this period. Directly across the road and up a short lane is the Cabbage Garden: now a beautiful park, this was once a Huguenot cemetery. Their historic headstones are still neatly displayed. The Deanery, where Jonathan Swift lived, is divided from the police station by St Patrick's Close.

Turn into St Patrick's Close. Note the old horse trough against the footpath and Marsh's Library and St Patrick's Cathedral ahead.

Marsh's Library

3 MARSH'S LIBRARY

Founded in 1701 by Archbishop Marsh, it is the oldest public library in Ireland with books dating back to 1472. The patrons' reading cages (to prevent pilferage) are still in place.

4 ST PATRICK'S CATHEDRAL

This ancient and famous cathedral would have collapsed from disrepair but for the generosity of brewer Sir Benjamin Lee Guinness who restored it in the 1860s. His statue is just inside the railings next to the entrance. The atmosphere created by the bells of St Patrick's and by nearby Christ Church is worth savouring any Sunday.

Turn right into Patrick Street passing St Patrick's Park where just inside the gate is a small plaque indicating the site of St Patrick's Well where the saint is reputed to have baptised the locals. Next to the park is a housing complex which includes the ornate, former Bull Alley Play Centre. The Guinness family built all of this and laid out the park for the poor of Dublin. Cross the road and enter Back Lane to view Tailors' Hall.

5 TAILORS' HALL

Tailors' Hall is the headquarters of An Taisce, the National Trust for Ireland. It is one of Dublin's few remaining Queen Anne buildings (erected in 1706) and is the city's oldest surviving guildhall.

Leave Back Lane and cross over High Street (the old Viking main street) to compare the 12th-century Protestant church with its Catholic counterpart (mid-19th-century). Both are named after St Audeon. The difference between street levels separated by seven centuries is visible through a window in the Catholic churchyard.

St Patrick's Cathedral, where Jonathan Swift was Dean for over 30 years, was intended to rival Christ Church – hence Dublin's two ancient cathedrals

Walk towards Christ Church, first passing the Synod Hall, now a tourist and community centre (its tower dates from an earlier church). Notice the connecting arched walkway with the cathedral itself.

6 CHRIST CHURCH

The excavated ruins beside the main door are the remains of an Augustinian Priory suppressed after the Reformation. Built in the late 12th century this great edifice also faced ruin in the last century and was saved by the distiller, Henry Roe. The crypt, perhaps Dublin's oldest structure, dates from 1172.

Leave Christ Church and cross the road, with a view of St Werburgh's Church, and enter Castle Street. Ahead is the City Hall and to the right, Dublin Castle.

7 DUBLIN CASTLE

Begun by King John in 1204, Dublin Castle has been much altered. Recent years have seen millions of pounds spent on restoring Dublin Castle to its earlier elegance and excavating it to show the 13th-century castle foundations, with a view to making it Ireland's centre for EEC Presidency sessions.

After the castle view in turn the City Hall, the Sick and Indigent Roomkeepers Society building (Dublin's oldest charity) in Palace Street and the Olympia Theatre across the road. Walk into Dame Street to see some notable financial institutions, including the modern Central Bank which caused a furore when it was built in the 1970s.

The walk ends by Trinity College.

OUT OF CITY

*Greystones, less than an hour's drive from the city—set
between the sea and the Wicklow Mountains, Dublin is in
easy reach of beautiful scenery and peaceful places*

AVONDALE HOUSE

Rathdrum, Co Wicklow 99 T18
Just 40 miles from Dublin, via
Rathnew, Avondale was the
birthplace in 1846 of the patriot and
social reformer Charles Stewart
Parnell. The house, built in 1779 to
James Wyatt's design, is now a
forestry school, open to visitors in
summer when the hall, sitting room
and Blue Room, with its fine
plasterwork, may be viewed. They
contain furniture and other items
associated with Parnell.

The forest park of 523 acres is
mainly on the west bank of the
Avondale River. There are picnic
sites and two signposted nature
trails. The house is open every day
during the height of summer
including afternoons on Saturdays
and Sundays.

AVOCA

Co Wicklow 99 T27
Avoca, 44 miles from Dublin, has
been scarred as a beauty spot by
industry—it has copper, lead and
zinc deposits—but its valley,
celebrated in Tom Moore's song *The
Meeting of the Waters*, is still
enchanting. About three miles north
of the picturesque village, the Avoca
River is formed by the confluence of
the Avonmore and Avonbeg, and
they mingle in a setting of sylvan
beauty. Croneblane, formerly Castle
Howard, crowns a cliff on the east
bank. Its former entrance, the Lion
Bridge, affords a striking view.

Near the 'meeting' is the leafless
skeleton of Tom Moore's Tree,
railed around to deter souvenir
hunters. The poet is said to have
spent many hours sitting under it.
The valley looks best in late spring,

Avondale contains a Parnell museum

when drifts of wild white cherry
blossom stand out against the
prevailing green. It is also a
convenient centre for visiting
Glenmalure, Lough Tay, Lough
Dan and other beauty spots. At
Woodenbridge, two miles south of
Avoca, is a second 'Meeting of the
Waters', the Aughrim and Avoca
rivers, at the junction of the Avoca,
Aughrim and Arklow valleys. There
is a nine-hole golf course at
Woodenbridge.

BALBRIGGAN

Co Dublin 97 O26
A small seaside town with a tiny,
quaint fishing harbour and a long
sandy beach, Balbriggan is 20 miles
north of Dublin and is a quiet resort
with a nine-hole golf course. The
beach is sheltered both north and
south of the town and there is pretty
coastal scenery. At Gormanston,
three miles north, is Gormanston
Castle (1786), a former seat of the
Preston family, with a 1687 chapel
from a previous castle. Now owned
by the Franciscans, it has a spherical
tea-house of yew trees. At
Bettystown, a little further north,
where there is an 18-hole golf
course, the Tara Brooch (see
National Museum, page 50) was
found on the beach in 1850.

BALLSBRIDGE

See Royal Dublin Society (page 56).

BOYNE VALLEY

See Brugh na Boinne.

BRAY

Co Wicklow 99 O21
A popular resort, with its mile-long
promenade terminating at the
landmark of Bray Head (791ft) at its
southern end, Bray is largely a
creature of the 19th-century railway
age, when day excursions brought
thousands from Dublin, 12 miles
north. Its perennial popularity stems
from its position between the capital
and the beauties of the Wicklow
Mountains.

Bray has a nine-hole golf course
and the Woodbrook championship
links are just to the north. The town
has an indoor heated swimming
pool and amusement arcades, and
there are walks along the Dargle
river in the harbour area and a fine
cliff walk southward of about five
miles to Greystones (occasionally
blocked by rock falls). *Oldhamia*, the
oldest fossil found in Ireland, occurs
at the base of Bray Head, and from
the summit of the Head are excellent
views. The town has attractive
streets, with views of the Great
Sugar Loaf (1659ft) to the south.

Kilruddery House, 1½ miles from
Bray, is an 1820 Elizabethan-style
mansion built for the Earl of Meath
by William Morrison. The Glen of
the Dargle, about 2½ miles from the
town, is a lovely deeply-wooded
defile with a jutting Lovers' Leap.

BRUGH NA BOINNE

Co Meath 97 O07
East of Slane and 32 miles from
Dublin are the prehistoric passage
graves of the Boyne Valley:
Newgrange, Dowth and Knowth,
all within sight of each other and
collectively called Brugh na Boinne.

There are at least 12 smaller
passage graves in the district and the
area was probably first called Brugh
na Boinne (Boyne Palace) on the
assumption that Tara's kings were
buried there, but the graves were
many centuries old before these
chieftains reigned. Across the Boyne
is Ross na Righ where King Cormac
MacAirt asked to be buried because
he considered the Newgrange side a
'cemetery of idolators'.

Knowth is not yet open to the
public. It has a wonderfully lavish
circle of kerbstones around the
mound.

Newgrange
Newgrange is one of the best
examples of a passage grave in
Western Europe, and dates from
about 3000BC. It consists of a
passage and chamber with large
unmortared slabs for walls and roof.

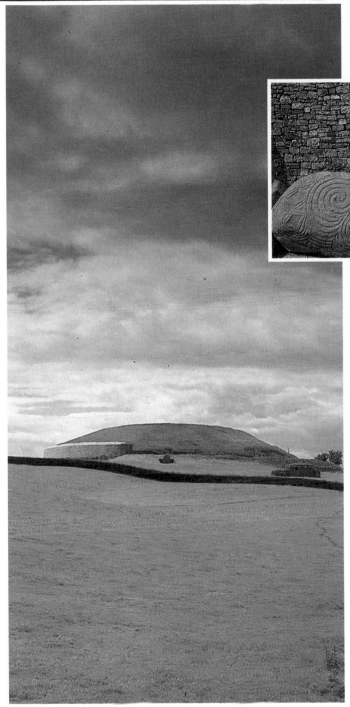

*Spirals and lozenge decorations (below) at
Newgrange (left). The mound is constructed
so that the sun's rays pierce the roof and
penetrate the chamber at sunrise on the winter
solstice. It is also well-drained – the chamber is
impressively dry*

Chamber

This is reached by a passage over
60ft long, containing 43 standing
stones. A tall slab standing near the
entrance was originally a door. The
chamber is 16½ft in diameter. Three
side chambers open off it, so that the
tomb's accessible area, including the
passage, has the shape of a high
cross. The chamber's vault, just
under 20ft from the ground at its
centre, is intact after nearly 5,000
years, and is considered the finest of
its kind in Europe. Four large basin-
shaped stones, two in the right-hand
recess and one each in the end and
left-hand recesses, contained the
burnt bones of the people whose
tomb this was. They had probably
been cremated elsewhere. Also
placed in the stones were beads,
pendants and brooches.

Newgrange is open every day
during the summer months, and
otherwise from Tuesday to Saturday
and Sunday afternoons.

Dowth

The chamber at Dowth was opened
in 1847 by Royal Irish Academy
archaeologists, when human and
animal bones, bracelets, brooches,
glass and amber beads and iron tools
were found. Both Dowth, which is
several hundred years younger than
Newgrange, and Newgrange itself
had been looted by Norsemen in
AD861, so we do not know their full
original contents.

Grass and other greenery now
grow on the Dowth mound. Its
passage is 27ft long and similar to
that of Newgrange, and its central
chamber, 9ft by 7ft and 11ft high in
the centre, is a rough circle, but side
chambers again give an overall
cruciform shape. Dowth also has
inexplicable carvings of circles,
spirals, zigzags and lozenges. A
stone circle and military rath are
nearby.

Dowth is not for the unfit, as
some crawling is necessary to view it
properly. It is open from June to
September. Instructions are given
for obtaining the key at other times.

A circular mound of stones covers
the tomb, and a kerb of massive
slabs laid on edge—some splendidly
decorated with spirals, lozenges and
other prehistoric motifs—
surrounds the base of the mound.

Encircling the mound at a
distance of up to 16 yards are tall
standing stones. Only 12 survive
from the original number of about
35. The circle encloses about two
acres. The first four stones, opposite
the entrance, are the largest, and
stand up to 8ft above the original
ground level. Most of the others
have been broken off near the
ground. The mound is 36ft high at
the front and is made of pebbles,
with white quartz stones used as a
dressing layer. The kerb, enclosing
just over an acre, consists of 97
stones up to 15ft long, many of them
decorated with carved spirals,
circles, zigzags and diamond-shapes,
or lozenges, whose meaning (if any)
is unknown. The entrance stone has
the most notable decorations.

Roof box

The only one of its kind, this small
box rests on the front part of the
passage roof about 8ft from the
entrance. It was discovered during
excavations in 1963. On 21
December, the winter solstice, and
only then, the rising sun's rays
penetrate the chamber through a slit
in the box's floor. The box is
beautifully decorated on the outer
edge.

Castletown House, the most important, architecturally, of its period

CASTLETOWN HOUSE

Celbridge, Co Kildare 99 N93
One of the most magnificent houses in Ireland, Castletown is 13 miles west of Dublin and is joined to the end of Celbridge's main street by an avenue of limes. It was built in 1722 for William Conolly, Speaker of the Irish House of Commons, and its architect was Alessandro Galilei, who designed the façade of Rome's St John Lateran basilica. A three-storey, 13-bay central block is joined by curved colonnades to two pavilions, one wing containing kitchens, the other stables. Castletown's print room is the only one of its kind in Ireland, and was created by Lady Louisa Conolly, who also commissioned the Francinis to do stucco-work on the house. The most striking room in the house is the Long Gallery, decorated in 1775.

The vista at the back of the mansion is closed by Conolly's Folly, an obelisk standing on arches designed by Richard Cassels, who worked on nearby Carton House, in 1740. Conolly's descendants lived in Castletown until 1965. The Festival of Music in Great Irish Houses is held here in June.

Castletown House is open throughout the entire year but opens on afternoons only on Saturdays and Sundays during the months of winter.

Celbridge Abbey, now a school for the mentally handicapped, was once the home of Esther Von Homrigh, Swift's 'Vanessa'.

The crossings made from Coliemore Harbour to Dalkey Island are well rewarded by the beauty of the coastline

DALKEY

Co Dublin 99 O22
Nine miles south-east of Dublin and at the entrance to Dublin Bay two miles beyond Dun Laoghaire, Dalkey consists primarily of the old town and a number of charming hillside villas. From Sorrento Terrace and Sorrento Park are splendid views of Killiney Bay. There are remains of two of the seven castles which guarded the harbour and town in medieval days, and near the town hall are the ruins of St Begnet's Church. Fragmentary ruins of the saint's oratory exist on Dalkey Island, largest of a group of offshore islands, which is crowned by a Martello tower. An annual burlesque ceremony of crowning a 'King of Dalkey Island' was begun in the 18th century and revived in 1935, but enthusiasm has waned.

There is a choice of several rock-enclosed pools for swimming, as well as a designated public pool. Dalkey Quarry is popular with rock-climbers. Most of the granite used to build Dun Laoghaire harbour came from here. Dun Laoghaire golf course and the nine-hole course at Killiney are both two miles away.

Torca Cottage on Dalkey Hill was the summer home of George Bernard Shaw from 1866 to 1874. As a 12-year-old he started a huge gorse fire on Torca Road.

DROGHEDA

Co Louth 97 O07
An historic port at the mouth of the Boyne, Drogheda today is a bustling place. It was first settled by Vikings in AD911, and in 1649 became the scene of a terrible massacre by Cromwell's army.

Good Georgian buildings can be seen in Drogheda, which still has one of its town gates, St Laurence's Gate, with two towers. St Peter's Church, West Street, has 13th-century remnants of St Mary's Abbey. It also has the head of St Oliver Plunkett.

A large grass mound with a wall is the Millmount, a prehistoric burial mound used by Vikings for ceremonies and as a castle 'motte' by Hugh de Lacy in the 12th century.

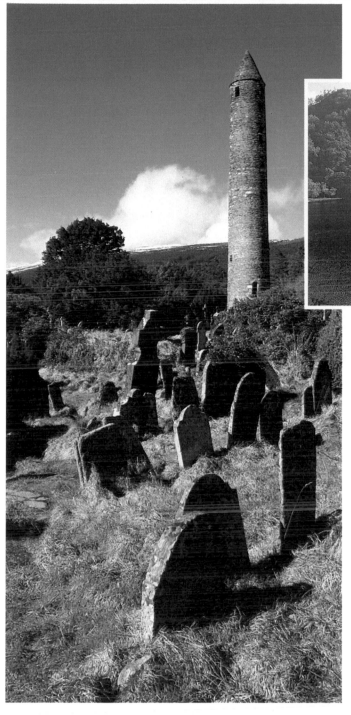

Glendalough's Upper Lake (above): the earliest monastic sites are found on its south side. The round tower stands near the only surviving early Irish monastery gatehouse

Ireland only in Norman times, having been brought to Europe by returning crusaders.

St Laurence O'Toole was a later administrator of Glendalough, before becoming Archbishop of Dublin in the 12th century.

The Teampall na Scellig on the Upper Lake's south shore, accessible only by boat, is an oratory of St Kevin, with a double-light east window cut from a single stone. Reefert Church at the south-east corner of the same lake consists of a nave and chancel. St Kevin's Cell, a little west, is the ruin of a beehive cell. The Caher, on this lake's eastern shore, is a ruin of a Bronze Age or early Iron Age stone fort. The gateway of the monastic city survives and the 110ft round tower is almost perfect. To its west is Our Lady's church, with massive west doorway, where St Kevin was buried. The 'Priests' House' is an attractive 12th-century Irish-Romanesque edifice rebuilt in 1779.

The Cathedral, largest of the ruins and dating from the 7th century, has some beautiful scroll carvings. St Kevin's Church (or 'kitchen') is a barrel-vaulted oratory whose round tower belfry was added in the 11th century. St Kieran's Church was forgotten until found under a mound of earth and stones in 1875. It commemorates the founder of Clonmacnoise. St Saviour's Priory, ¾ mile east of the cathedral, is probably of the late 11th century and was rebuilt in about 1875. Trinity Church, about the same distance north-east of the cathedral, is said to have been the Church of St Mocherog, grandson of Brachan, King of Britain, and a close friend of St Kevin.

GLENDALOUGH

Co Wicklow 99 T19
Glendalough is 32 miles south of Dublin. Literally the 'glen of two lakes' and a place of wild beauty hemmed in by precipices and steep flanks, it is rich in ruins of a monastic city which flourished from the early 6th century until 1398 when it was burnt and deserted. Chosen by St Kevin as a solitary retreat, it drew disciples around him until his hermitage had grown into a monastery; it later became a renowned seat of learning. It suffered the usual Norse raids, was devastated by a great flood in 1174 and later took the brunt of fighting

between Wicklow chiefs and Anglo-Normans before its final demise.

St Kevin is said to have slept in a tree hollow and in a 7ft by 4ft cave 30ft up a rock face overlooking the Upper Lake; the cave, 3½ft high, is still called St Kevin's Bed. Visitors still hear the story of how the saint was pursued to this glen by 'beautiful red-headed Kathleen with eyes of unholy blue' and threw her from a cliff into the lake; in an alternative version he rolls her and himself in nettles to cool their ardour. Early male Irish saints are often presented in legend as outrageous misogynists, but a flaw in this yarn is that the name Kathleen (Katherine) reached

*Howth Peninsula—coast walks,
birdwatching and good views*

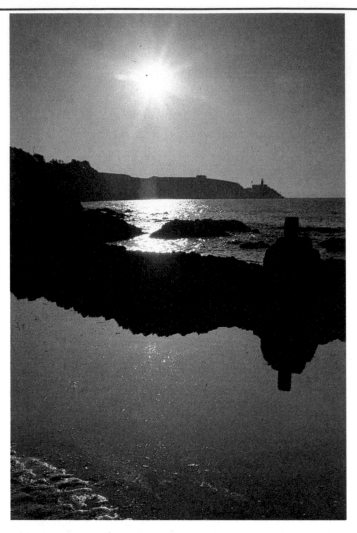

GREYSTONES

Co Wicklow 99 O21
On a pleasantly wooded part of the
Wicklow coast 18 miles south of
Dublin, this small town still has
something of the air of the former
quiet fishing village, though it has
become enormously popular not
only to visit but to live in. Wide
tree-lined roads and well-planned
modern residences add to its
attraction. As a resort, with fine
sandy beach, its specialities are
bathing, fishing and boating, but
there is also a choice of two 18-hole
golf courses at the Greystones and
Delgany clubs. Delgany, an
attractive village among trees a mile-
and-a-half from Greystones, is itself
less than a mile from the beautiful
ravine called Glen O' the Downs.

HOWTH

Co Dublin 97 O23
Howth Castle gardens are noted for
their beauty, in particular for a
remarkable collection of 2,000
varieties of rhododendrons, many of
great rarity. Nine miles from the city
centre, Howth peninsula forms the
north-east extremity of Dublin Bay.
It rises to 550ft and its high parts
give fine views of the islands of
Ireland's Eye and Lambay to the
north, with the Mourne Mountains
beyond visible on clear days. To the
west the long sweep of the North
Bull Island is seen running back
towards the city. There is a bird
santuary here. The best vantage
points are in the hilly grounds of
Howth Castle, a short distance west
of the harbour, which are open daily
all year; the rambling castle is not
open. The St Lawrence (now
Gaisford-St Lawrence) family has
lived here since 1177, but the oldest
parts of the present castle are of the
14th century.

At the entrance to the half-mile
long, 30ft high beech hedge walk
planted about 1710, is an elm
planted in 1585, the oldest
introduced tree in Ireland. The
gardens are also noted for their
shrubs. In the demesne is a massive
dolmen called Aideen's grave.
Nearby are the ruinous remains of
Corr Castle, and tiny St Fintan's
Church with both early and
medieval remains.

Howth village, a popular
suburban resort, is noted for its
fishing fleet. There is an interesting
cliff walk ascending from
Balscadden and going around the
peninsula; for golfers, Howth Golf
Club has an 18-hole course and there
is also a Sutton club.

JAPANESE GARDENS

Tully, Co Kildare 98 N71
Just outside Kildare town in the
National Stud grounds, 34 miles
south-west of Dublin, the gardens
were devised by Lord Wavertree
and laid out (1906—1910) by the
Japanese garden designer Eida and
his son Minoru to symbolise the life
of a man. There is a signposted
route. A cavern in a mound of rock
symbolises life's beginning, a tunnel
represents the ignorance of
childhood and the Hill of Learning
is crowned by a tall pine. The
Parting of the Ways is at a triple
fork, a smooth part to the right
(carefree life), a narrow one to the
left (bachelorhood) and stepping
stones straight ahead which lead to
married life. Two bridges over a
stream represent engagement and
marriage. A Honeymoon Path is
broad, for husband and wife to walk
abreast, and an obstruction
symbolises the first quarrel. Further
on are the Hill of Ambition, Tea
House, miniature Japanese village,
Well of Wisdom, Red Bridge of
Life, smooth path to the Chair of
Old Age, Hill of Mourning and
Gateway to Eternity, surrounded by
weeping trees.

The beautiful gardens may be
enjoyed for their own sake, without
becoming involved in the
symbolism. They contain a
charming pagoda, a Japanese
restaurant and a souvenir shop.
There are occasional wrestling
displays.

The gardens are open daily from
Easter to October (Sunday
afternoons only).

JOYCE MUSEUM

Dun Laoghaire, Co Dublin 99 O22
Nine miles south-east of Dublin on
the coast road, the museum is
housed in a thick-walled Martello
tower where James Joyce was the
guest of Oliver St John Gogarty
before leaving Ireland. *Ulysses* opens
in this tower, with Gogarty in the
character of Buck Mulligan. The
museum is devoted to items
associated with Joyce, including
some manuscripts and a piano and
guitar which he played. The roof,
with gun rail still in place, may be
visited. Nearby is a 'gentlemen only'
bathing place named the Forty-
Foot, which has been defiantly
visited by women's rights activists.

The museum is open daily during
the summer months (Sunday
afternoons only).

KELLS (CEANANNUS MOR)

Co Meath 96 N77
Among the historic remains in this interesting town – renowned source of *The Book of Kells* (see page 64) – are a 100ft-high roofless Round Tower, 9th-century St Columcille's House, high-roofed with 4ft-thick walls, and five ancient high crosses. A few miles north-west of Kells is a 14th-century Church of St Kieran and, nearby, the saint's Holy Well.

KILLINEY

Co Dublin 99 O22
Killiney Bay, 11 miles south-east of Dublin, affords one of the country's most beautiful views, especially when seen from the summit of Killiney Hill, easily reached from Vico Road and laid out as a public park. As well as the two-mile crescent beach, Bray Head, the Great and Little Sugar Loaf and distant Howth Head can be seen from here. The summit is crowned by a 1741 obelisk and on the hill's south side is the ancient ruined Killiney Church, with a curious collection of stones called the Druid's Chair.

The beach is a favoured bathing, fishing and boating area, and the White Rock strand to its north is equally popular. There is a nine-hole golf course.

MALAHIDE CASTLE

Malahide, Co Dublin 97 O24
Eight miles north of Dublin in grounds of 250 acres, the castle was owned by the Talbot family from 1185 to 1976. Despite inevitable changes, it still has a 14th-century core, and the small entrance and narrow stairs are further evidence of antiquity. Much of the National Portrait Collection from the National Gallery is on display here, including those of the Talbot family, James Gandon and a self-portrait of Nathaniel Hone the Elder. The Great Hall, Oak Room and two drawing rooms may be seen. There are 16th-century Flemish and Dutch carvings, and Dutch furniture of the 17th century. The castle contains an antique shop and there are picnic areas in its park.

The castle is open daily all year (Sunday afternoons only); Saturday afternoons only during the winter months.

Lived in by the Talbot family for 800 years, Malahide Castle is the home of much of the National Portrait Collection from the National Gallery

The obelisk folly on Killiney Hill was built in 1741

MOUNT USHER GARDENS

Ashford, Co Wicklow T29
These gardens, 28 miles south of Dublin on the River Vartry, downstream from the Devil's Glen, are privately owned and date from about 1860. They contain many magnificent trees and shrubs, some of great rarity, including 70 species of eucalyptus, a few of which are immense. There are Montezuma pines, tall eucryphias which are covered in blossoms from ground to tip in season, southern hemisphere beeches, the rare Brewer's weeping spruce, Chilean crocus, the New Zealand 'Ti tree' and the *populus maximowiczii*, covered at times with innumerable 10-inch catkins. One of the eucryphias here is the gardens' own hybrid.

The gardens have been developed by the Walpole family since Edward Walpole first planted the land surrounding an old corn mill. They have spread from one acre to almost 20. Leading horticulturists Sir Frederick Moore, Sir John Ross, E A Bowles and others advised on their early development, and they now include azalea, lime, and palm walks, a holy well, a wishing well and a croquet lawn, and four bridges and five weirs on the Vartry. There is a carriage museum with over 50 restored horse-drawn vehicles.

The gardens are open daily during the summer.

NATIONAL MARITIME MUSEUM

Dun Laoghaire 99 O22
Eight miles south-east of Dublin on the coast road, the museum is in the 1837 Mariners' Church, with an anchor carved in stone over the door at Haigh Terrace. The centrepiece of its display is an 1865 optical system from the Baily lighthouse in Howth, across Dublin Bay, still in working order. Also here is a 35ft French longboat captured in Bantry Bay, Co Cork, in 1796, and believed to be the world's oldest surviving ship's boat.

The museum is famed for its model collection, which includes a 9ft representation of the *Great Eastern*, Isambard Kingdom Brunel's 'great iron ship', which ended its career as an Atlantic cable-layer and was captained by Robert Halpin of Wicklow. Brunel coincidentally designed a railway viaduct not far from Dun Laoghaire. Models also include a Limerick Steamship Company freighter lost with all hands on the Lisbon run in 1943, Irish Shipping freighters, the Wexford Steamship Company's coaster *Kerlogue* which crossed the Atlantic during World War II, and even a Guinness Liffey barge, with barrels.

NATIONAL STUD

Tully, Co Kildare 98 N71
Outside Kildare town, 34 miles
south-west of Dublin, the stud
adjoins the Japanese Gardens (see
page 86) and was founded by the
same man, Lord Wavertree. It
passed from his ownership to that of
the British Government, and in the
1940s was transferred to the Irish
Government. Stallions are bought
from all over the world, the number
usually kept here varying from six to
ten. The eccentric Lord Wavertree
liked to arrange matings between
stallions and mares to suit births of
foals under his chosen signs of the
Zodiac, and Tully's stalls are built to
facilitate the study of heavenly
bodies.

The Irish Horse Museum at the
National Stud traces the evolution
of horses, its centre-piece being the
skeleton of the legendary jumper
Arkle. The many artefacts on
display include jockey Pat Taaffe's
silks and Celtic chariot wheels.
There is also a hunting section.

The stud has daily guided tours
from April to October. Security is
understandably strict. The museum
is open daily from April to October
(Sunday afternoons only).

*Factory floor for a major Irish industry –
mares and foals at the National Stud (main
picture and above right). Right: skeleton of
Arkle, three-times winner of the Cheltenham
Gold Cup, 1964 to 1966, at the Irish Horse
Museum*

The formal terraces at Powerscourt took from 1745 to 1867 to complete. Beyond is the cone of the Sugarloaf Mountains. Right: detail of the vine leaf pattern ironwork in the Venetian Gate at Powerscourt.

NEWGRANGE

See Brugh Na Boinne (page 82).

POWERSCOURT DEMESNE

Enniskerry, Co Wicklow 99 O21
Powerscourt is 13 miles south of Dublin and the estate's gardens are some of Ireland's finest. Among their glories are a superb array of trees some, including giant beeches, over 200 years old. The great mansion, formerly owned by the Wingfields (Powerscourts) was designed by Richard Cassels about 1730, incorporating part of an ancient castle; it was badly burned some years ago, but the beauty of the gardens remains. These, both formal and informal, are embellished by much elegant ironwork, urns, statuary and a pepper pot tower. The terraces, commanding a spectacular view of the Great Sugar Loaf mountain, are a special feature, the top one being 800ft long. The Triton Pool with its 60ft fountain is the centre-piece, and the wrought iron is from a castle in Hamburg. A formal Italian garden, a walled English garden and a Japanese garden are among the attractions.

Powerscourt waterfall, at 400ft possibly the tallest in the British Isles, is reached by a winding rhododendron drive, and falls from a rocky cleft. The Dolphin Pond, surrounded by huge eucalyptus trees, is another spectacular sight. The estate is open daily during the summer months; the waterfall may be seen all year.

RUSSBOROUGH HOUSE

Blessington, Co Wicklow 99 N91
Richard Cassels died while working on this Palladian masterpiece for Joseph Leeson MP, son of a wealthy Dublin brewer and later Lord Milltown. The work, begun in 1741, was completed by Francis Bindon. The plasterwork, much of it by the Francini Brothers, is superb, and the house, 20 miles south-west of Dublin, is also notable for its Louis XVI furniture, 18th-century tapestries and a wealth of worked and moulded Caribbean mahogany. The Italian marble mantels by Thomas Carter, with panels

representing legends, are a special feature.

The house's Beit collection of paintings is now part of the National Trust. It was assembled between the late 1880s and 1906 by Alfred Beit, co-founder with Cecil Rhodes of the De Beers Diamond Mining Company, and includes works by Goya, Gainsborough, Rubens, Vermeer and Velazquez. Beit's nephew became owner of Russborough.

Russborough is open Sunday and Bank Holiday afternoons from Easter to October, and every day in high summer. There are woodland gardens.

SKERRIES

Co Dublin 97 O26
Skerries is a hugely popular seaside resort 19 miles north of Dublin, noted for a dry, bracing climate and a sandy beach. Many Dublin families rent accommodation here for the entire summer. There is a nine-hole golf course and boating and tennis are available. At Red Island, now on the mainland, St Patrick is said to have begun his mission and indentations in the rock are said to be his footprints. Ireland's first holiday camp was established here.

Offshore are three small islands: St Patrick's, Colt and Shenick's, the last-named accessible on foot at low tide. St Patrick's Island, also called Church Island, has an ancient church ruin. Barnageeragh Bay, just over a mile north-west of the town, is a favourite picnic spot. The cliff walk south of the town leads to the pretty bay of Loughshinny, a small fishing village. Skerries itself also has an established fishing industry. Two miles south-west are St Moibhi's oratory and holy well (7th century), and two miles south of the town are the well-preserved ruins of Baldungan Castle, scene of a 1642 massacre by Parliamentary forces.

Skerries still has a busy fishing fleet as well as being a popular resort

Swords' towers: 6th-century round and 14th-century square

SWORDS

Co Dublin 97 O14
Eight miles north of Dublin, Swords is a straggling little town at the centre of an area of varied interest. St Colmcille (Columba) founded a monastery here in the 6th century; this has vanished, but Swords Castle (built in about 1200), a large irregular pentagon, still stands at the northern end of the town. A 75ft round tower stands in the grounds of the Protestant church, and another nearby tower is the remnant of a medieval church.

At Lusk village, five miles north, are another round tower and ancient church. Two miles east of here is Rush, a quiet seaside place popular with families because of its safe bathing, and noted for market gardening, as the greenhouses

testify. Three miles offshore is Lambay Island, a noted bird sanctuary owned by Lord Revelstoke. Special permission is needed to go there, and may be applied for to the island's steward in Rush.

South-east of Swords via Malahide (see Malahide Castle, page 87) is St Doulagh's Church, on the site of the anchorite cell of St Doulagh (who lived around AD600). The present Church of Ireland parish church is an 1864 rebuilding, but there is an ancient stone-roofed chapel. Also here are a 14th-century tower and an ancient baptistry built over a well.

TRIM CASTLE

Trim, Co Meath 96 N85
Trim stands on the Boyne 28 miles north-west of Dublin. The huge, 16-sided castle keep, 75ft tall, still visually dominates its surroundings despite many years of neglect. It originally had 20 sides, and even in its shrunken form appears what it was, the biggest Anglo-Norman fortress in Ireland. The keep was built (1190—1200) by Hugh Tyrell, out of rough limestone with some sandstone trimmings, and stands on a central mound in an enclosed area

of two acres, the outer wall being about 500yd long. This wall was strengthened by ten circular towers, including those at the gates. Most of these survive and date from 1220. , The unique south gate, with barbican, is well preserved; in its tower, in 1399, Henry of Lancaster, later King Henry V, and his cousin Humphrey of Gloucester were imprisoned for a time by Richard II. The Normans held parliaments in the castle and 'Silken' Thomas Fitzgerald occupied it for a time during his brief revolution (1534—36), despite its intimidating defences.

Visitors should follow Castle Street to the river, turn right and climb a timber stile to enter the castle area. A second stile is negotiated in order to view all sides of the keep. From here it is impossible not to notice the 125ft Yellow Steeple across the river, a remnant of the 13th-century St Mary's Augustinian Priory. The Steeple survived both the Ironsides' guns and later the deliberate blowing up of the Priory to prevent Cromwellian occupation. The decay of Trim Castle began with these same guns.

Trim: a fine surviving example of Irish medieval military architecture

MAPS & DRIVES

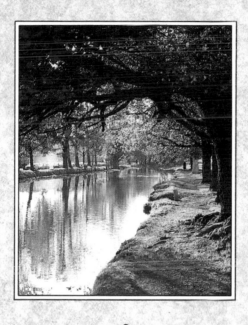

The Grand Canal, linking Dublin Bay with the Shannon,
winds through the southern outskirts of Dublin. Patrick
Kavanagh, the poet, wrote of its 'leafy—with—love' banks

Islands, Coast and Country

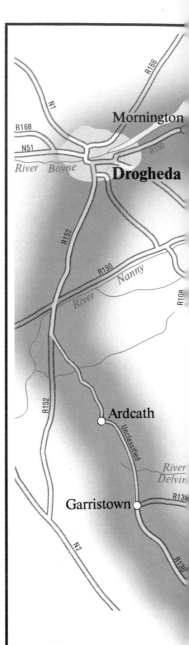

Amost attractive drive along the coast north of Dublin, which affords fine views of the many small and rocky offshore islands. The route turns at bustling Drogheda where there is much for the visitor to enjoy, from the Millmount, a huge prehistoric grass mound, to a fine 19th-century viaduct across the River Boyne. The drive returns to Dublin through gentle farming countryside.

From the north-east side of Dublin city centre leave by the Fairview and Clontarf Road. Pass through the northern suburbs and drive alongside the shore of Dublin Bay. After 4 miles pass the Bull Wall on the right. This leads to the interesting Bull Island Bird Sanctuary, and there are views of the Howth peninsula ahead. *In 3¾ miles, at some traffic lights, turn right with the R105, signed Howth Head, and gradually ascend to the summit of Howth Head.* A road from the Summit Inn leads to a car park which affords good views over Dublin Bay to the distant Wicklow Hills.

Descend to **Howth** (see page 86), *enjoying fine seascape views which include a small island known as Ireland's Eye. Continue to Howth Harbour and turn left, then after ¼-mile pass the entrance to medieval Howth Castle.* A short detour can be made round its pleasant gardens. *In 1¼ miles at traffic signals turn right, still with the R105, signed Baldoyle. Drive over a level crossing, and in ¼-mile reach Baldoyle. Turn right here, then after a further 1¼ miles turn right again on to the R106 for the resort of Portmarnock.* The fine expanse of sandy beach here is known as the Velvet Strand.

Continue along the coast towards Malahide, with seaward views of Lambay Island, the remnant of an ancient volcano. Enter **Malahide** *and keep forward through the town.* A visit to the castle here is well worthwhile (see page 87). *In 1 mile turn right, signed Swords. Stay inland and pass through agricultural country.* The ancient village of **Swords** was an important foundation of St Columba and a detour can be taken to see its few remaining ruins (see page 90*). At the edge of the village take the third exit at the bypass roundabout on to the main Dublin/Belfast road (N1) then after 3¾ miles turn right on to the R127 signed Skerries. In another 2 miles bear right into the village of Lusk. Turn right on to the R128 Rush road and enter* the market-gardening area for Dublin.

Proceed to Rush and turn left signed Skerries. Rejoin the coast and follow a section of the drive which affords seaward views of the Rockabill lighthouse, with Shenick's Island in the foreground. *Enter* **Skerries**, *turn left at the obelisk, then go forward at the crossroads.* Skerries (see page 89) is a popular seaside resort with a good sandy beach and the ruins of an early 12th-century monastery. *Turn right signed Balbriggan on to the R127 and continue* along the coast, with views of the distant Mourne Mountains.

Enter **Balbriggan** (see page 82), *cross a railway bridge, then turn right signposted Drogheda. Still in the town, turn right to rejoin the N1 and drive inland.* Cross the county border just beyond the town and enter Co Meath. *Proceed to Julianstown, and on an ascent turn right on to the R150 signed Laytown, then in 1½ miles bear right. Rejoin the coast for the last time at Laytown and continue to Bettystown. Bear left here and left again signed Mornington, then in ¼-mile bear right signed Drogheda. After ¼-mile turn right, then in 1 mile keep left and immediately right. Continue to Mornington, turn left and follow* the Boyne Estuary to enter the historic town of **Drogheda** (see page 84). If time allows, a prolonged visit should be made to this archaeologically and historically important town.

Leave Drogheda via Mary Street, and at a T-junction turn left signed Dublin, then turn right on to the R152. In 5 miles branch left on to an unclassified road signed Ardcath/Garristown, and after another 2 miles turn left, then bear right and continue to Ardcath. At Ardcath keep left and drive through undulating farming country to *Garristown. Keep forward on to the R130 signed Dublin and in 1 mile bear left.* The Dublin Mountains can be seen in the distance. *In 5 miles go forward at a crossroads, then in 2¾ miles turn left on to the N2. After another 2¼ miles* pass a left turn leading to the National Monument of Dunsoghly Castle. This massive structure is situated on a small hillock in a marsh and dates from the 15th century. Its keep still retains the roof timbers and is flanked by four angle towers. *Continue through the built-up areas around Finglass, and return to Dublin through the suburbs.*

Home of the Talbot family for eight centuries, Malahide Castle still has its medieval Great Hall and keep. The castle is also the home of much of the National Gallery's National Portrait Collection

A popular resort and busy fishing harbour, Skerries is on the coast where St Patrick may have begun his mission

Howth takes its name from the Norse for headland. It was once an island, linked over the millennia to the mainland shore

Boyne Estuary

Bettystown

Laytown

lianstown

N1

Delvin

River

R122

Balbriggan

R127

Skerries

Shenick's Island

R127

R128

N1

F108

R132

Lusk

R127

R128

Rush

R130

N1

R125

Swords

Malahide

River

Ward

River

R108

R106

Portmarnock

VELVET STRAND

Ireland's Eye

R107

R106

M1

Baldoyle

R105

Howth

DUNSOGHLY CASTLE

R104

R105

HOWTH CASTLE

N2

Finglas

North Bull Island

BIRD SANCTUARY

River

Tolka

DUBLIN

Dublin Bay

N3

BULL WALL

River Liffey

Around the Sugarloaf

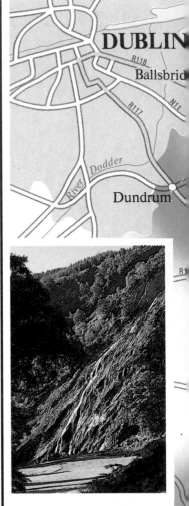

A picturesque tour around the Great and Little Sugarloaf Mountains, crossing the Rivers Dargle and Glencullen. The drive allows detours to the attractive village of Bray and to Powerscourt House, with its beautiful gardens.

Leave Dublin by the R118 and in 2¼ miles reach Ballsbridge. The **Royal Dublin Society** complex is seen to the right (see page 56). *Three miles from Ballsbridge, at the resort of Blackrock, branch left on to an unclassified road signed Dun Laoghaire and in ½-mile turn left signposted Dun Laoghaire Pier.* From here there are fine views across Dublin Bay and the magnificent granite-built Dun Laoghaire harbour, designed by John Rennie.

Beyond the car ferry go forward signed Dalkey. *Drive along the seashore and in 1¼ miles turn right at a T-junction.* The left turn here leads to the Forty-Foot bathing place for men and **Joyce Museum** (see page 86). *In 100yds turn left at a crossroads on to the R118 signed Dalkey, and in ½-mile pass Bullock Castle on the approach to* **Dalkey** (see page 84). *Turn left at a T-junction into Castle Street. At the end bear right signed Killiney into Railway Road, then bear left into Sorrento Road. In ¾-mile turn right into Vico Road.* Ascend with views of Dalkey Head behind and **Killiney**, Bray and Bray Head visible ahead. Pass wooded Killiney Hill (see page 87), surmounted by an obelisk, and *in ¼-mile turn left signposted Coast Road, Bray. In ¼-mile go forward at a staggered crossroads, and after another ½-mile turn left on to the R119. In ¼-mile keep forward with the main road, then in ¾-mile go forward on to the N11 to pass through Shankhill. In 1¾ miles keep forward on to the R767 then cross the River Bray to enter* **Bray** (see page 82).

Drive through the town, branching right at a sign Glendalough/Roundwood. In 1¾ miles turn right on to the N11 dual carriageway, signed Dublin, and in ½-mile turn left on to the R117 and continue along the wooded Glencullen River valley to Enniskerry. Turn left, signed Powerscourt, then on reaching a clock tower, bear left on to the R760 to climb past the entrance to **Powerscourt Demesne** *(on the right) (see page 89).*

In ¾-mile bear right: both the Great and Little Sugarloaf Mountains can be seen ahead. *After 1 mile turn left on to the R755 and descend through fine rocky scenery with the Great Sugarloaf (1654 ft) on the right. Drive to Kilmacanoge and turn right on to the N11 signed Wexford. In 2 miles enter the Glen of the Downs and shortly pass the access to the Bellevue Woods* – with nature trails and a picnic site – *on the left.*

Two miles farther pass the edge of Kilpedder, from where the lower slopes of the Wicklow Mountains can be seen to the right. *In 1½ miles pass Newtownmountkennedy, and in 5 miles turn right on to an unclassified road signposted Roundwood. In ½-mile turn right on to the R764. At a crossroads in ¾-mile keep forward to pass through a gap between low hills, and continue to the edge of Vartry Reservoir; bear right on to an unclassified road signed Sally Gap. Follow the shores of the reservoir, and in 1½ miles turn left on to the R765. In ½-mile, at the edge of Roundwood, turn right on to the R755 and in a further ½-mile turn left signed Sally Gap, Enniskerry. Continue straight for 1½ miles and* you will see Djouce Mountain rising to 2385 ft on the left. *In 3¾ miles pass Djouce Wood on the left,* and shortly obtain a fine view over Bray Head and the coast to the right.

Some ¾-mile beyond this point, turn left signed 'Waterfall'. Descend steeply along a narrow road and in ¼-mile turn left at a crossroads to continue the descent. In ½-mile pass the access to Powerscourt Waterfall (on the left) and bear right across the Dargle River, signposted Glencree. Climb through the forest, then after 5½ miles at the 1300 ft head of Glencree Valley, turn right (R115) signed Rathfarnham. A view to the right extends down the Glencree Valley to the distant Great Sugarloaf. *In ¼-mile branch right (signed Glencree) and descend to the area known as Glencree. Descend gradually below Prince William's Seat (1825ft) on the left, with pleasant views across the valley.*

Drive past Curtlestown Church (on the left) 3¼ miles from Glencree. In 1¼ miles bear left signed Glencullen and cross the Glencullen River. Keep forward at the Glencullen crossroads (signed Stepaside) to a 1000 ft summit below Two Rock Mountain (1763 ft). In ¾-mile descend, with views over Dublin Bay. *After another 2 miles turn left on to the R117.* Continue to Dundrum; go forward at the crossroads. Follow signs to City Centre for Dublin.

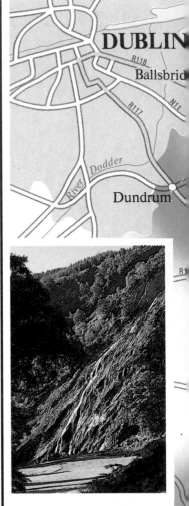

Powerscourt Waterfall, where the Dargle River plunges several hundred feet

The 1654ft summit of the Great Sugarloaf, reflected here in the waters of the Vartry Reservoir

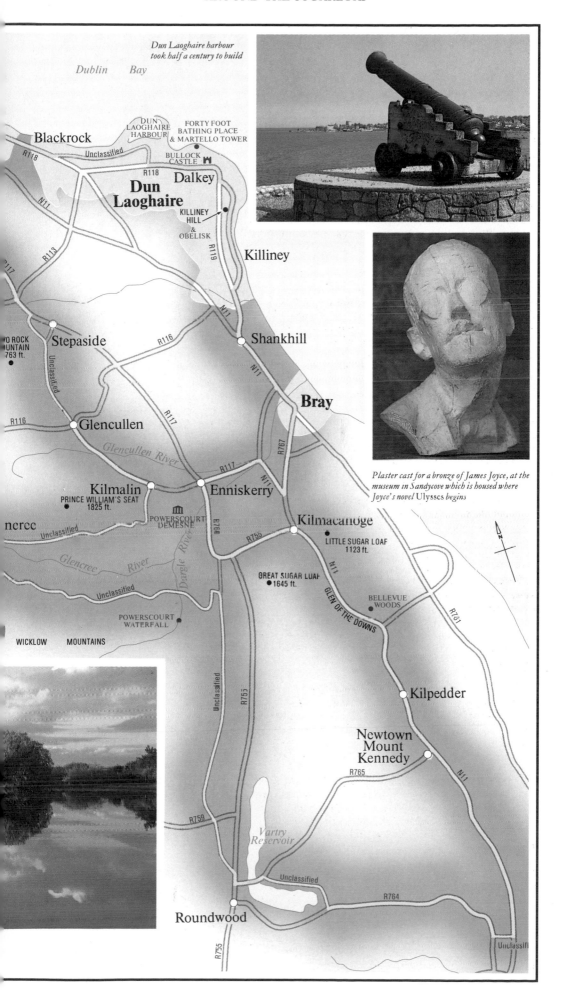

Dun Laoghaire harbour took half a century to build

Dublin Bay

Blackrock

DUN LAOGHAIRE HARBOUR

FORTY FOOT BATHING PLACE & MARTELLO TOWER

BULLOCK CASTLE

R118

Dalkey

Dun Laoghaire

KILLINEY HILL & OBELISK

Killiney

R119

R118

N11

R113

R117

Stepaside

O ROCK UNTAIN 763 ft.

R116

Unclassified

Shankhill

R116

Glencullen

N11

Bray

Glencullen River

R117

R767

Kilmalin

PRINCE WILLIAM'S SEAT 1825 ft.

Enniskerry

POWERSCOURT DEMESNE

R117

N11

ncrcc

Unclassified

Glencree River

Dargle River

R768

Kilmacanoge

LITTLE SUGAR LOAF 1123 ft.

R755

GREAT SUGAR LOAF 1645 ft.

BELLEVUE WOODS

GLEN OF THE DOWNS

N11

Plaster cast for a bronze of James Joyce, at the museum in Sandycove which is housed where Joyce's novel Ulysses begins

POWERSCOURT WATERFALL

WICKLOW MOUNTAINS

Unclassified

N

R761

R753

Kilpedder

Unclassified

Newtown Mount Kennedy

R765

N11

R759

Vartry Reservoir

Unclassified

Roundwood

R764

R755

Unclassifi

SLIGO 136

BALLINA
153

N4

BOYLE
109

N57

SWINFORD
135

N5

CARRICK-ON-SHANNON
100

CASTLEBAR
152

N60

WESTPORT
163

N60

N5

ROSCOMMON
91

N60

N63

TUAM
120

R332 (L4)

N63

R363 (L4)

R362 ATH
(L4)

N6

GALWAY
136

N6

BALLINASLOE
94

LEGEND

M1	Motorway
N6	National Primary Route
N60	National Secondary Route
R752 (T7) R332 (L4)	Regional Roads
	Motorway Junction
128	Distance in miles to Dublin

PORTUMNA
103

R489 (T41)

BIR
87

ENNIS
146

N7

NENAGH
98

New York 6hrs 55mins

N68

N18

N7

KILKEE
180

N67

SHANNON AIRPORT
139

N19

N18

THUR
9

LIMERICK
123

N69

N69

N20

BALLYBUNION
176

R551 (L105)

N69

CASHEL
99

N21

N74

TIPPERARY
112

N21

N8

TRALEE
188

N21

CASTLEISLAND
177

N23

MITCHELSTOWN
128

N73

N22

N72

MALLOW
149

FERMOY
138

KILLARNEY
192

DUBLIN

N71

N8

KENMARE
213

CORK
160

N25

YOUGHAL
144

N2

Key to Places of Interest

1 Abbey Presbyterian Church	D8
2 Abbey Theatre	E7
3 Aldborough House	F8
4 Bank of Ireland	D6
5 Belvedere House	C8
6 Bluecoat School	A6
7 Brazen Head Hotel	A5
8 Casino Marino	F8
9 Chester Beatty Library and Gallery of Oriental Art	F4
10 Christchurch Cathedral	B5
11 City Hall	C5
12 Custom House	E7
13 Dublin Castle	C5
14 Dublin Civic Museum	D5
15 Eccles Street	C8
16 Four Courts	B6
17 Gaiety Theatre	D4
18 Gate Theatre	D8
19 General Post Office	D7
20 Government Buildings	E4
21 Grand Canal	A1-F2
22 Guinness Brewery	A5
23 Iveagh House	D3
24 Kilmainham Jail	A5
25 King's Inns	B8
26 Leinster House	E4
27 Mansion House	D4
28 Marsh's Library	B4
29 Mountjoy Square	E8
30 Municipal Gallery of Modern Art	C8
31 Museum of Childhood	C1
32 National Botanic Gardens	B8
33 National Gallery of Ireland	E4
34 National Library	E4
35 National Museum	E4
36 Olympia Theatre	C5
37 Phoenix Park	A6
38 Powerscourt House	D5
39 Pro-Cathedral	D8
40 Prospect Cemetery	B8
41 Rathfarnham Castle	A1
42 Rotunda Hospital	D8
43 Royal Canal	
44 Royal College of Surgeons	
45 Royal Dublin Society	
46 Royal Hospital	A5
47 St Andrew's Church	
48 St Ann's Church	
49 St Audoen's Churches	
50 St Catherine's Church	
51 St Francis Xavier Church	
52 St George's Church	
53 St Mary's Church	

102

Street Index with Grid Reference

Central Dublin

Key to Town Plan

- AA Recommended roads
- Restricted roads
- Buildings of interest — Station ▪
- Churches — †
- Car Parks — Ⓟ
- Parks and open spaces
- AA Service Centre — AA

Street scene near the Four Courts, on the River Liffey

The following pages contain practical information including opening times.
ADDRESSES IN DUBLIN
The postal district number is given after the street name. Odd postal numbers (1, 3, 5 etc) are north of the city, even numbers are south.

TELEPHONE NUMBERS
A six-figure number is usually given, which is correct for phone calls within the Dublin area. If calling Dublin from elsewhere in Ireland, use the prefix *01* before the number. If calling from outside Ireland, use the appropriate international dialling code (for example, *0001* from the UK).

The information in this Directory is liable to change at short notice. While every effort has been made to ensure that it is comprehensive and up to date, the publishers cannot accept responsibility for errors or omissions, or for changes in the details given.

How to Get There

Dublin Airport is served by major international airlines from the United Kingdom, Europe and North America, and has internal flights. Competition between airlines makes short trips feasible—for golf, fishing or sightseeing—as well as longer holidays. The airport is about seven miles from the city centre and is served by the 41A bus or the Airport Bus Service from the Central Bus Station (Busaras).

Both the B & I Line and Sealink operate Cross Channel ferry services between Dublin and Britain on a daily basis. Their passenger offices sit cheek by jowl in Westmoreland Street, Dublin 2. For B & I information, telephone *778271*; Sealink, telephone *808844*.

Entry Requirements
Visas are not generally required to get into Ireland except from a small number of countries such as the USSR, Cuba and Libya. Anyone coming from a place outside the State, other than Great Britain or Northern Ireland, must be in possession of a valid passport or other document of equal validity.

Accommodation

If you come for the Horse Show, then a Dublin 4 address will probably get you closest; for shopping and city centre sights, Dublin 1 and 2 (central addresses north and south of the Liffey) will be convenient. A Room Reservation Service is provided by Dublin & East Tourism.

Unless otherwise indicated by (ER)—Egon Ronay recommended—all the *Hotels* and *Guesthouses* listed here are AA recommended.

The *Hostels* listed here are not AA recommended, but are approved by the Tourist Board. They are included as acceptable basic accommodation.

AA Classifications

Hotels

★★ Hotels with a good standard of accommodation. There should be 20% private bathrooms or showers

★★★ Well-appointed hotels. Two thirds of the bedrooms should have private bathrooms or showers

★★★★ Exceptionally well-appointed hotels offering high standards of comfort and service. All bedrooms should have private bathrooms or showers

T & C Town and Country Homes are regularly inspected and meet minimum criteria

Restaurants

✕ Modest but good
✕✕ Higher standard of comfort than above
✕✕✕ Well-appointed
✕✕✕✕ Exceptionally well-appointed restaurant

Rosettes indicate that the cuisine is of a higher standard than is expected in an establishment within the classification. Red stars indicate outstanding merit within the classification.

For more details and latest information on hotels, guesthouses and restaurants please see the current editions of the *AA Members' Handbook—Ireland* and Egon Ronay's annual *Hotel and Restaurant Guide*, where the respective hotel and restaurant symbol rating systems are explained.

HOTELS

Berkeley Court (ER), Landsdowne Rd, 4 *Tel 601711*
★★★★**Burlington**, Leeson St, 4 *Tel 605222*
★★★★**Jury's**, Ballsbridge, 4 *Tel 605000*
★★★★**Shelbourne**, St Stephen's Green, 2 *Tel 766471*
Westbury (ER), off Grafton St, 2 *Tel 791122*
★★★**Ashling**, Parkgate St, 8 *Tel 772324*
★★★**Blooms**, Anglesea St, 2 *Tel 715622*
★★★**Dublin International** (at Dublin Airport 6m N on N1) *Tel 379211*
Gresham (ER), O'Connell St, 1 *Tel 746881*
★★★**Hotel Montrose**, Stillorgan Rd, 4 *Tel 693311*
★★★**Marine** (at Sutton 8m N on coast road R106) *Tel 322613*
★★★**Royal Dublin**, O'Connell St, 1 *Tel 733666*
★★★**Sach's**, Morehampton Rd, 4 *Tel 680995*
★★★**Skylon**, Upr Drumcondra Rd, 9 *Tel 379121*
★★★**Tara Tower**, Merrion Rd, 4 *Tel 694666*

DUN LAOGHAIRE

★★★**Royal Marine** *Tel 801911*
★★★**Hotel Victor**, Rochestown Av, *Tel 853555*
T & C Ferry, 15 Clarinda Park North *Tel 808301*

HOWTH

★★**Howth Lodge** *Tel 390288*

KILLINEY

★★★**Court** *Tel 851622*
★★★**Fitzpatrick's Castle** *Tel 851533*

MALAHIDE

★★★**Grand** *Tel 450633*

GUESTHOUSES

Abrae Court, 9 Zion Rd, Rathgar, 6 *Tel 979944*
Ariel House, 52 Landsdowne Rd, 4 *Tel 685512*
Beddington, 181 Rathgar Rd, 6 *Tel 978047*
Burtenshaw's 'Marian', 21 Upr Gardiner St, 1 *Tel 744129*
Eagle Lodge, 12 Clontarf Rd, 3 *Tel 336009*
Egan's, 7 Iona Pk, 9 *Tel 303611*
Iona House, 5 Iona Pk, 9 *Tel 306217*
Mount Herbert, 7 Herbert Rd, 4 *Tel 684321*
St Aidan's, 32 Brighton Rd, 6 *Tel 902011/906178*
St Jude's, 17 Pembroke Pk, 4 *Tel 680483*

HOSTELS

An Óige, The Irish Youth Hostel Association, 39 Mountjoy Sq, 1 *Tel 745734*
Open Apr—Oct
Morehampton House, 78 Morehampton Rd, 4 *Tel 680325*
Open all year
Bookings for all An Óige Hostels must be made through their head office in Mountjoy Sq (see above), and payment made in advance. Sleeping bags essential; self-catering kitchens available.

OTHER HOSTELS

Tourist Board approved:
YWCA Radcliffe Hall, St John's Rd, Sandymount, 4 *Tel 694521*
More a good-value guesthouse; Bus No 3 goes to the door. Open all year except Xmas
Isaac's, 2–5 Frenchman's Lane, 1 *Tel 749321/787227*
Self-catering kitchens and restaurant.
Open all year, 24 hours a day
The Young Traveller, St Mary's Place, 7 *Tel 305000/381553*
4-bedded rooms, each with shower, towels, soap, sheets and duvet supplied; restaurant, coin-operated launderette, TV lounge.
Open all year, 24 hours a day

Eating and Drinking Out

The most memorable Irish meals are likely to be those which have been cooked with care and respect for their incomparable raw ingredients and served relatively unadorned. Great meals (whatever their cooking method) will probably have one or other of the following in them somewhere: shellfish, smoked salmon, fresh salmon (January to August), sea trout, roast beef, fresh brown bread, hot scones.

Pubs are as much a part of Irish life as churches and betting shops, and more than anything else in this country attract an astonishing cross-section of people.

The pubs in the list which follows may or may not have Irish Music (see *Entertainment*, page 110, for those that do) but they are all traditional in the sense that Dubliners gather in them as a matter of course. But a listing such as this must be subjective.

Unless otherwise indicated by (ER)—Egon Ronay recommended—the *restaurants* listed here are AA recommended. The *pubs* and *coffee shops* which follow are not AA recommended, but are included as traditional and acceptable Dublin venues.

❀✕✕✕✕**Le Coq Hardi,** 35 Pembroke Rd, 4 *Tel 689070*
❀✕✕✕**Celtic Mews,** 109a Lower Baggot St, 2 *Tel 760796*
✕✕✕**Ernie's Mulberry Gdns,** Donnybrook, 4 *Tel 693300*
✕✕✕**Killakee House,** Killakee Rd, Rathfarnham, 16 *Tel 932645*
✕✕✕**Locks,** 1 Windsor Ter, 8 *Tel 752025*
❀✕✕✕**The Lord Edward,** 23 Christchurch Pl, 8 *Tel 752557*
Mitchell's Cellars (ER), 21 Kildare St, 2 *Tel 680367*
❀✕✕✕**Patrick Guilbaud,** 46 James's Pl, 2 *Tel 764192*
✕✕**Kapriol,** 45 Lower Camden St, 2 *Tel 751235*

✕✕**Old Dublin,** 91 Francis St, 8 *Tel 751173*
✕✕**Rajdoot Tandoori,** Westbury Centre, Clarendon St, 2 *Tel 794274*
✕**Quo Vadis,** 15 St Andrew Street, 2 *Tel 773363*
❀✕✕✕**Whites on the Green,** 119 St Stephen's Green, 2 *Tel 751975*

DALKEY

✕✕**Guinea Pig** *Tel 859055*

DUN LAOGHAIRE

Digby's (ER), 5 Windsor Terrace *Tel 804600*
❀✕✕✕**Restaurant Na Mara,** Crofton Rd *Tel 806767*
✕✕✕**Restaurant Mirabeau,** Marine Parade, Sandycove *Tel 809873*

HOWTH

❀✕✕✕**King Sitric** *Tel 325235*

MALAHIDE

❀✕✕**Johnny's,** 9 St James Ter *Tel 450314*

TRADITIONAL PUBS

An Béal Bocht, 58 Charlemont St, 2
Music nights; probably the only cash register in the city that gives receipts in Irish.
The Bailey, Duke St, 2
Brazen Head Inn, 20 Lr Bridge St, 8
First got its licence in 1666; probably the oldest pub in the city.
Davy Byrne's, 21 Duke St, 2
A stopping point in Leopold Bloom's trek on 16 June 1904.
Doheny & Nesbitts, 5 Lr Baggot St, 2
Complete with 'snugs'; attracts barristers, journalists, fiercely loyal regulars.

Joxer Daly's, 103 Dorset St, 1
Lovely pub noted for its lunches and snacks.
Kitty O'Shea's, 23 Upper Grand Canal St, 4
Delightful-looking pub with traditional music nights.
McDaid's, Harry St, 1
A famous literary drinking spot for Dublin's bygone literati; now jammed with types who always have a book in progress but never seem to finish.
Mulligan's, 8 Poolbeg St, 2
Looks its 200 years; ambience lends itself to an extraordinary sampling of Irish life.
Neary's, 1 Chatham St, 1
Not everyone's idea of a traditional pub but comfortably plush and central, with convenient loos.
O'Donoghue's, 15 Merrion Row, 2
The king of all traditional pubs with music of the 'bring your own' variety; one of the most genial hosts in the country.
The Old Stand, 37 Exchequer St, 2
Backslapping sporty types; lovely pub.
William Ryans, 28 Parkgate St, 8
Beautifully-fitted pub off the beaten track, sometimes targetted by the trend-setters about town.
Scruffy Murphy's, 1 Powerscourt, Lr Mount St, 2
Stylish mix of sociable singles and regulars.
Slattery's, 129 Capel St, 2
A favourite for music enthusiasts; traditional, folk and blues.
The Stag's Head, 1 Dame Court, 2
Difficult to find but worth it— best approached from Exchequer St. A relaxed 200-year-old pub and a large cast of regulars.
Toner's Victorian Bar, 139 Lr Baggot St, 2
Highly sociable mix of students and artists.

COFFEE SHOPS

Bewley's, 78/79 Grafton St, 2; 12 Westmoreland St, 2; 13 South Great George's St, 2
Dublin's best-known rendezvous; irresistible aroma of coffee beans.
The Carriage Restaurant, The William Elliott Ctr, Wicklow St, 2

Excellent coffee, gateaux, soup, salads.
Club '76, Brown Thomas of Grafton St, 2
Good coffee; excellent gateaux.
The Kilkenny Shop, Nassau St, 2
Bright, airy café overlooking Trinity College's cricket ground; notable brown bread and salads.
National Gallery Restaurant, Merrion Sq, 2

Popular lunch and snack venue; open during gallery hours.
Next, Henry St, 1
Coffee counter inside the door; good vantage point from which to watch the motley pass.
The Shelbourne Hotel, St Stephen's Green, 2
Elegant stopping-point for morning coffee, afternoon tea; good for celebrity-spotting.

Places to Visit

Dublin city is a gift for anybody who likes walking and has time to spare. A large part of the city's attraction lies in its people; the warmth of the true 'Dubs', their gregariousness and willingness to help, are just as much a part of Dublin as Christ Church or Trinity College. Tourists who try to soak up the atmosphere from a coach window may be seeing the sights but they are missing the essential Dublin.

A popular way of seeing Dublin is through guided walks. Contact: Guided Walks into Old Dublin (Liberties), conducted by native Dubliners *Tel 556970/533423/532407*. Tour Guides Ireland, Glendenning Ho, Wicklow St *Tel 794291/794386*.

Brief descriptions are usually given only for places not elsewhere in the book. Otherwise, see pages 32–65 for more information on places in central Dublin and pages 82–89 for places outside. Admission is free except where stated.

ARCHAEOLOGY

Wood Quay, 8 Cradle of the city of Dublin, key to its Viking past, pulse of Viking city life between the 9th and 11th centuries, Wood Quay is now the site of blocks of civic offices, not erected without a struggle. The excavations revealed a mighty store of Viking artefacts, which may be viewed in the National and Civic Museums.
Open any time

OUTSIDE DUBLIN

Newgrange, Co Meath (Boyne Valley)
Open Jun–Sep, daily; Nov–Mar, Tue–Sat & Sun pm
Admission charge
Dowth, Co Meath (Boyne Valley)
Open Jun–Sep, daily
Admission charge

ART GALLERIES

Chester Beatty Library & Gallery of Oriental Art, 20 Shrewsbury Rd, 4 *Tel 692386*
Open Tue–Fri 10am–5pm, Sat

2–5pm. Free guided tours Wed & Sat, 2.30.
Hugh Lane Municipal Gallery of Modern Art, Charlemont Ho, Parnell St, 1 *Tel 741903*
Open Tue–Sat 9.30am–6pm, Sun 11am–5pm.
National Gallery of Ireland, Merrion Sq West, 1 *Tel 615133*
Open weekdays 10am–6pm, Thu till 9pm; Sun 2–5pm (& guided tours every half hour). Closed Xmas & Good Friday. Special bookings through Education Officer 2wks in advance. Bookshop & restaurant. Admission free; donations appreciated.
United Arts Club, 3 Upr Fitzwilliam St, 2 *Tel 762965*
Paintings by Irish artists. Open lunchtime and evenings; evenings only at weekends.

OUTSIDE DUBLIN

Portrait Gallery, Malahide Castle, Malahide, Co Dublin *Tel 452337/452706/452655*
Open Mon–Fri 10am–12.45, 2–5pm; Apr–Oct, Sat 11am–6pm, Sun & BHs 2–6pm; Nov–Mar, Sat, Sun, BHs 2–5pm
Restaurant. Admission charge

COMMERCIAL GALLERIES

Dublin has numerous examples: see Bord Fáilte Information Sheet No 37.

CATHEDRALS AND CHURCHES

Churches are open for services and at the times given below. They may be open at other times, but these are liable to change.

Abbey Presbyterian Church
Parnell Square, 1
Open for services (11am Sun).
Christ Church Cathedral, Lord Edward St, 8
Open Oct–Apr, Tue–Fri 9.30am–12.45pm, 2.15–4.30pm; Sat 10am–1pm; May–Sep, Mon–Sat 10am–5pm.
Contributions are invited.
Findlater's Church (see Abbey Presbyterian Church)

Pro-Cathedral, Marlborough St, 1
Mass is sung each Sunday at 11am by the Palestrina Choir.
St Andrew's Church, St Andrew's St, 2
Open for services.
St Ann's Church, Dawson St, 2
Open daily, all year. Admission charge for lunchtime recitals.
St Audoen's Church, High St, 8
Open Fri–Wed 11.30am–1.30pm
St Catherine's Church, Thomas St, 2
Not open.
St Francis Xavier Church, Gardiner St, 1
Open for services.
St George's Church, Hardwick Pl, off Temple St, 1 *Tel 305289*
Caretaker on duty Mon, Wed Sat.
St Mary's Church, Mary St, 1
Check with Tourist Information Centre (page 117).
St Mary's Pro-Cathedral (see Pro-Cathedral)
St Michan's Church, Church St, 8
Tours of church & vaults Mon–Fri 10am–12.45pm, 2–4.45pm; Sat 10am–12.45pm. Vaults closed Sun & Easter. Sunday service 10.30am. Admission charge.
St Patrick's Cathedral, Patrick St, 2
Open Mon–Fri 9am–6pm, Sat 9am–4pm, Sun at times of Divine Service. Contributions are invited.
St Werburgh's Church, Werburgh St (off Christ Church Place), 8 *Tel 720673*
Open Mon–Fri 10am–4pm by appointment. Sunday service 10.30am.
University Church, St Stephen's Green, 2
Open for services (masses daily).

CEMETERIES

Arbour Hill Cemetery, Arbour Hill, 7
Scene of many sombre wreath-laying occasions: the executed leaders of the Easter Rising in 1916 are buried here.
Open daily 9.30am–5.30pm.
Prospect Cemetery, Glasnevin, 9
Open daily, all year

HISTORIC BUILDINGS

'Not open' means that the building is not generally open to the public, although it is worth seeing from outside and may be open for functions or by invitation.

Bank of Ireland, College Green, 2 *Tel 776801*
   Open banking hours Mon–Fri 10am–12.30, 1.30pm–3pm (5pm Thu)

Belvedere House
   Not open.

Bluecoat School
   Not open.

Casino, Malahide Road, Marino
   Open 10am–7pm daily in summer (May–Sep approx); otherwise Sat 10am–4pm, Sun 2pm–4pm. Admission charge.

City Hall, Dame St, 2
   Open Mon–Fri 9am–1pm, 2.15pm–5pm.

Custom House
   Not open.

Dublin Castle, Dame St, 2
   Usually open Mon–Fri 10am–12.15pm and 2pm–5pm, Sat and Sun 2pm–5pm but check with a Tourist Information Centre (below). Admission charge.

Four Courts, Inns Quay, 8 *Tel 725555*
   Open (for those who would like to see Irish Justice meted out) Mon–Fri 11am–1pm, 2–4pm

General Post Office (GPO)
   O'Connell St, 1 *Tel 726666*.
   Open for business Mon–Sat 8am–8pm, Sun 10.30am–6.30pm.

Government Buildings
   Not open.

Guinness Hop Store
   (see *Museums*)

Irish Whiskey Corner, Irish Distillers, Bow St, 7 *Tel 725566*
   Old warehouse converted into exhibition centre with a relaxing bar for tasting sessions. The selling is indeed persuasive and Scotch-drinkers may be converted in spite of themselves. No tours for individuals, but you are welcome to join a party tour. Contact the public relations office. Take buses 21 or 78, or a taxi (it isn't easy to find).

Iveagh House
   Not open.

Kilmainham Jail Historical Museum, Kilmainham, 8 *Tel 535990*
   Open Jul–Sep, Wed & Sat 2–6pm; Oct–Jun, Sun 2–6pm. Admission charge.

King's Inns, Constitution Hill and Henrietta St, 1
   The park is open to the public. The building and library may be visited by arrangement with one of the Benchers of King's Inns.

Leinster House, Kildare St and Merrion Sq, 2 *Tel 789911*
   The public is admitted to the Dáil visitors' gallery only with an introduction from a Teachta Dáil (MP).

Mansion House
   Not open.

Rathfarnham Castle
   Not open.

Rotunda Hospital
   Parnell St and Sq, 1
   Parties may visit chapel by arrangement.

Royal College of Surgeons
   Not open.

Royal Dublin Society
   (See *Libraries*)

The Royal Hospital,
   Kilmainham, 8 *Tel 718666*
   Guided tours, concerts, exhibitions, and many other events. Restaurant (usually with entertainment). Admission charge.

Tailors' Hall
   Not open.

Trinity College, 2 *Tel 772941*
   Trinity belongs to all the people of Dublin and during the day the grounds are often used as a short-cut to different places. It is also a favourite place for a lunchtime run or just for sunbathing. *The Book of Kells* may be found in the Long Room of the Old Library; queues to see it are often horrendous. *The Book of Kells:* open Mon–Fri 9.30am–4.30pm, Sat 9.30am–12.30pm. Admission charge applies seasonally Apr/Oct.

Tyrone House
   Not open.

OUTSIDE DUBLIN

Avondale House, Rathdrum, Co Wicklow
   Open May–Sep, Mon–Fri 10am–1pm, 2–6pm; Sat & Sun 12noon–6pm. Admission charge.

Castletown House, Celbridge, Co Kildare
   Open Apr–Oct, 10am–5pm, Sat & Sun 11am–6pm (closed 1–2pm); Nov–Mar, Mon–Fri 10am–5pm, Sat, Sun & BH 2–5pm. Admission charge.

Malahide Castle, Malahide, Co Dublin *Tel 452655*
   Open all year, Mon–Fri 10am–12.45pm, 2–5pm; Apr–Oct, Sat 11am–6pm, Sun & BH 2–6pm; Nov–Mar, Sat, Sun & BH 2–5pm. Admission charge.

Newbridge House and Park, Donabate, Co Dublin *Tel 436534*
   Delightful mid-18th-century mansion filled with original furniture; the house appears more or less as it was 150 years ago. Coffee shop.
   Open Apr–Oct Mon–Fri 10am–5pm, Sun & Bank Hols 2–5.30pm. Closed weekdays 12.45–2pm, and all day Sat. Special opening for groups of 20 or more. Admission charge. Bus from Eden Quay; trains from Connolly Station with half-hour walk.

Russborough House, Blessington, Co Wicklow
   Open Easter–31 Oct, Sun & Bank Hols 2.30–5.30pm; and daily in Jul & Aug, 2.30–5.30pm. Admission charge.

LIBRARIES

Central Catholic Library, 74 Merrion Sq South, 2 *Tel 761264*
   Nearly 60,000 books and an unusual and comprehensive collection of Irish and foreign Catholic periodicals and newspapers, contemporary and retrospective.
   Open Mon–Sat 11am–7.30pm. Closed Sun. Free admission to visitors using the reference library.

The Chester Beatty Library and Gallery of Oriental Art (see under *Art Galleries*)

Dublin Public Libraries, Central Library, Ilac Centre, Henry St, 2 *Tel 734333*
   A wide range of services includes computer loan-recording, language learning centre, video-viewing, information services, micro-computer use, lending library, children's library, music and record library, business information services, newspapers (Irish and foreign, journals and periodicals). Also trade and telephone directories from around the world.
   Open Mon–Thu 10am–8pm; Fri–Sat 10am–5pm. Membership and services free of charge; small registration fee if you wish to join the record lending section.

Dublin Public Libraries, Administrative Headquarters, Cumberland House, Fenian St, 2 *Tel 619000* for information on other services.

Goethe-Institut (German Cultural Institute), 37 Merrion Sq, 2
   Cultural programmes; language courses and library.
   Open Mon, Tue, Thu 4–8pm; Wed & Fri 10am–6pm; Sat 10am–1pm.

King's Inn Library, Henrietta St, 1 *Tel 747134*
   Admission to members of Inns;

others by special permission only. Hours vary during Academic year.
Open Mon 2–6pm; Tue–Fri 11am–6pm; Sat 10am–1pm.

The National Library of Ireland, Kildare St, 2 *Tel 765521*
Open Mon–Thu 10am–9pm (5pm from mid-Jul to mid-Aug); Fri 10am–5pm; Sat 10am–1pm.

Marsh's Library, St Patrick's Close, 8 *Tel 753917*
Open Mon 2–4pm; Wed, Thu & Fri 11am–12.30pm, 2–4pm; Sat 10.30am–12.30pm. Closed Tue & Bank Hols.

Royal Dublin Society Library, Ballsbridge, 4 *Tel 680645*
Admission to members only. Open Tue & Fri 10am–5pm, Wed & Thu 10am 7pm, Sat 11am–5pm. Closed Mon.

Royal Irish Academy Library, Dawson St, 2 *Tel 764222*
Houses one of the most extensive collections of ancient Irish MSS in this country, including *The Book of the Dun Cow*—history and romances of pre-Christian and Christian periods written on ancient vellum. Open Mon 9.30am–7.45pm (Jul & Sep 9.30am–5.15pm); Tue–Fri 9.30am–5.15pm. Closed Bank Hols & first 2 weeks of Aug.

Trinity College Library (see *Historic Buildings*)

University College Libraries, Belfield, Upper Merrion St, Earlsfort Ter and Shelbourne Rd *Tel 693244*
Open Mon–Fri 9am 10pm, Sat 9am–1pm. Hours vary during vacations.

MUSEUMS

Civic Museum, 58 South William St, 2 *Tel 794260*
Open Tue–Sat 10am–6pm, Sun 11am–2pm. Guided tours Wed 1.15pm.

Guinness Hop Store, Crane St, 8 *Tel 536700*
Sample a glass of Dublin's finest and take a look at Ireland's first brewing museum, with a cooperage display and transport gallery. Beautifully restored sampling area, ideal for relaxing, interesting place.
Open Mon–Fri 10am–3pm.

Irish–Jewish Museum, 3/4 Walworth Rd, 8 *Tel 534754*
Irish–Jewish memorabilia, documents, photographs etc. Earliest records 160 years old; housed in old synagogue.
Open Sun 10.30am–12.30pm; May–Oct, Mon & Wed 11am–3.30pm. Bus: 15A/B, 47/47B.

Museum of Childhood, The Palms, 20 Palmerston Pk, Rathmines, 6 *Tel 973223*
Open Jul & Aug, Tue–Sun 2–5.30pm; Sep, Nov–Jun, Sun 2–5.30pm. Closed Oct. Admission charge.

The National Museum, Kildare St, 2 *Tel 765521*
Open Tue–Sat 10am–5pm, Sun 2–5pm. Admission charge applies to Treasury Section, except Tue.

National Wax Museum, Granby Row, 1 *Tel 746416*
Not a national institution in spite of its name. Life-size figures of Irish people of historical, political, acting and sporting note. Chamber of Horrors.
Open Mon–Sat 10am–5.30pm, Sun 1–5.30pm. Admission charge.

Pearse Museum, St Enda's Pk, Rathfarnham, 14 *Tel 905208*
The family home of patriot Padraic Pearse and his brother Willie, where they later founded an Irish boys' school. The founding of the school, the brothers' nationalistic politics (which led to the use of the school as a holding point for arms), the 1916 Rising and Pearse's eventual execution with 15 others, are all documented in a 20-minute audio-visual show. The house has been restored and many documents, photographs and Pearse family memorabilia are on display.
Open May–Aug 10am–12.30pm & 2–6pm; Mar, Apr, Sep & Oct until 5.30pm, Jan & Dec until 3.30pm. Feb & Nov until 4.30pm.

RTE Broadcasting Museum, 27 Lr Rathmines Rd, Portobello, 6 *Tel 932798*
Early wireless and TV receivers, phonographs, musical boxes, etc. laid out in part of a church.
Open mornings by appointment. Bus: 15

OUTSIDE DUBLIN

Howth Transport Museum, Howth Castle, Howth, Co Dublin *Tel 475623/480831*
Fire engines, lorries, trucks, tractors and other vehicles, including the celebrated Hill of Howth No 9 Tram.
Open Sat, Sun & Bank Hols 2–6pm. Admission charge.

James Joyce Museum, James Joyce Tower, Sandycove, Dun Laoghaire, Co Dublin *Tel 809265/808571*
Open Apr–Oct, Mon–Sat 10–5pm (closed 1–2pm), Sun 2.30–6pm. Admission charge.

National Maritime Museum, Haigh Ter, Dun Laoghaire, Co Dublin *Tel 800969*
Open 1 May–Sep, 2.30–5.30pm every day except Mon (open Bank Hols). Admission charge.

National Stud, Tully, Co Kildare
Open daily, Apr–Oct, guided tours. Museum open Apr–Oct, Mon–Fri 10.30am–5pm, Sat 10.30am–5.30pm, Sun 2–5.30pm. Admission charge.

OBSERVATORY

Dunsink Observatory, Dunsink, Co Dublin *Tel 387911/387959*
Dunsink is one of the oldest observatories in the world and includes a 12in refractor, in the South Telescope, built by Grubb's of Dublin in 1863, which is used on Open Nights if the sky is clear. Exhibits.
Open Sep Mar, 1st & 3rd Sat 8–10pm. Admission free but tickets must be obtained by sending a stamped, addressed envelope to the Secretary. Children under 12 are courteously discouraged.

PARKS & GARDENS

National Botanic Gardens, Glasnevin, 9
Open Mon–Sat 9am–6pm, Sun 11am–6pm in summer; Mon–Sat 10am–4.30pm in winter. Greenhouses open shorter hours.

Phoenix Park, 7
Open any time

St Enda's Park Rathfarnham, 14 (see also Pearse Museum under *Museums*)
Twenty-five acres of parkland up against the Dublin Mountains; a leaflet from the museum will guide you along the Wayfarer nature trail, so-called after Pearse's poem.
Open daily, 10am–dusk. Bus: 16, 47B

St Stephen's Green, 2
Open Mon–Sat 8am to dusk, Sun 10am–dusk

OUTSIDE DUBLIN

Howth Castle, Howth, Co Dublin
Grounds open daily all year, 8am–sunset. Admission charge

Japanese Gardens, Tully, Co Kildare
Open Etr–Oct, Mon–Fri 10.30am–5pm, Sat 10.30am–5.30pm, Sun 2–5.30pm. Admission charge

Mount Usher Gardens, Ashford, Co Wicklow
Open 17 Mar–31 Oct, daily 9am–5.30pm. Admission charge Admission charge

Powerscourt Demesne, Enniskerry, Co Wicklow
Open 17 Mar–31 Oct, daily 9am–5.30pm. Admission charge

St Anne's Park, Mount Prospect Ave, Clontarf, Co Dublin
Avenues of trees, playing pitches, woodland, a rose garden, bridges, archways and a lake.
Open daily. Bus: 30 or 44A, or take the Dart to Killester

ZOO

Zoological Gardens, Phoenix Park, 7 *Tel 771425*
Open Mon–Sat 9.30am–dusk, Sun from 11am. Admission charge

Entertainment

Nightclubs, with few exceptions, double as discos and are basically extensions of pub life which closes down by law at 11.30pm (11pm in winter). Drinks may be expensive. Visiting cabaret artistes are rare but Dublin gets more than its fair share of visiting top-class rock groups and singers on the world circuit. It can also claim a lively array of home-grown talent.

The National Concert Hall provides a magnificent setting not only for home and visiting classical musicians, but also for folk, jazz, dance and many other forms of entertainment.

Dublin has a wide selection of first-class cinemas and a pub culture that needs no elaboration except to specify those that feature Irish traditional music and ballads on a regular basis.

What most visitors find astounding however (and something which Dubliners tend to take for granted) is the sheer diversity and quality of Irish theatre. Each theatre has its own identity, but the one any tourist will probably want to see is the Abbey – the Irish National Theatre.

September sees the annual celebration of the Dublin Theatre Festival, a two- sometimes three-week packed programme that attracts a dynamic array of international companies and, in the best tradition, goes on against awesome financial odds.

Programmes of events for the major venues are usually available from tourist offices and department stores such as Switzers and Brown Thomas; the National Concert Hall publishes a monthly calendar of events. Best source of information on every activity going on in the city is *In Dublin* magazine, a fortnightly publication that comes out on Thursdays; or see the evening newspapers.

CABARET

Some of these are dinner shows; some give an option. Check when booking.
Abbey Tavern, Howth, Co Dublin *Tel 390307/322006*
Braemor Rooms, County Club, Churchtown, 14 *Tel 988664/ 981016/982308*
Clontarf Castle, Castle Avenue, 3 *Tel 332271/332321*
Doyle's Irish Cabaret, Burlington Hotel, Upr Leeson St, 4 *Tel 605222* (May–October)

Embankment City, Saggart, Co Dublin *Tel 516116*
Jurys Irish Cabaret, Jurys Hotel, Ballsbridge, 4 *Tel 605000* (May–October, 6 nights a week)
Sheiling Hotel, Howth Rd, Raheny, 5 *Tel 314222*

CINEMAS

Adelphi, Mid Abbey St, 1 *Tel 731161*
Ambassador, Parnell Sq, 1 *Tel 787530*
Cameo, Mid Abbey St, 1 *Tel 730249*
Carlton, Upr O'Connell St, 1 *Tel 731609*
Curzon, Mid Abbey St, 1 *Tel 730438*
Green, St Stephen's Green, 2 *Tel 751753*
Odeon, Eden Quay, 1 *Tel 744611*
Savoy, Upr O'Connell St, 1 *Tel 748487*
Screen, College St, 2 *Tel 714988*
German Film Club, Goethe Institute, Merrion Sq, 2 *Tel 611155*
Spanish Film Club, Spanish Cultural Institute, 58 Northumberland Rd, 4 *Tel 682024*

CONCERT HALLS

Classical music recitals are also held in churches and halls around the city.

The National Concert Hall, Earlsfort Ter, 2 *Tel 711888; 711533* (credit card bookings) An Events Listing for the Concert Hall is available each month from the NCH, Tourist Offices and other outlets, and see also newspapers.

DISCOS/NIGHTCLUBS

Annabel's, Burlington Hotel, 4 *Tel 605222* (Full licence)
Flamingo's, Parkes Hotel, Stillorgan, Co Dublin *Tel 881621* (Full licence)
Hooray Henry's, Powerscourt Townhouse Centre, 2 *Tel 794742*
Club Nassau, Kildare St, 2 *Tel 605244* (Full licence)
Pink Elephant, South Frederick St, 1 *Tel 775876*
Tamango's, Sands Hotel, Portmarnock, Co Dublin *Tel 460003/460107* (Full licence)

JAZZ

Jazz in Dublin takes the form of regular weekly sessions in pubs and

hotels around the city. Some have a cover charge. For latest session details check *In Dublin* or evening newspapers.

NIGHTCLUBS

In a city where nightclubs open with a flourish and die with a whimper, to try listing them all would be foolish. The following is just a sample of those which appear to be there to stay.

Annabel's (see *Discos*)
Bojangles, 26 Lr Leeson St, 2 *Tel 789428*
Hooray Henry's (see *Discos*)
Le Cirque, 16 Merrion Rd, 2 *Tel 602236*
Parkers, 38 Lr Leeson St, 2 *Tel 765620*
Pink Elephant (see *Discos*)
Samantha's, 33 Lr Leeson St, 2 *Tel 765252*
Strings, Lr Leeson, 2 *Tel 613664*
Suesey Street, 25a Lr Leeson St, 2 *Tel 686674*

ROCK

Major rock concerts in Dublin usually take place at **The RDS,** Ballsbridge, 4 and **The National Stadium,** South Circular Rd, 8. For concert information and/or tickets, see Concert Tickets under *Shopping* (page 111).

There are also a number of venues around the city noted for nurturing up-and-coming, as well as established, rock talent; the Baggot Inn, 143 Lr Baggot St (*Tel 761430*) is one of them. For others, see *In Dublin*.

THEATRES

Abbey and Peacock Theatres, Lower Abbey St, 1 *Tel 787222*
Centre for the Performing Arts, 39 Ormond Quay Lr, 1 *Tel 734597*
Dublin Theatre Festival, 47 Nassau St, 2 *Tel 778439*
Dublin University Players, 4 Trinity College, 2 *Tel 774673*
Focus Theatre, 6 Pembroke Place, 2 *Tel 763071*
Gaiety Theatre, Sth King St, 2 *Tel 771717*
Gate Theatre, 1 Cavendish Row, 1 *Tel 744045/746042*
Lambert Puppet Theatre, Clifton Lane, Monkstown, Co Dublin *Tel 800974*
Olympia Theatre, Dame St, 2 *Tel 778962*
Project Arts Centre, 39 East Essex St, 2 *Tel 712321*

TRADITIONAL MUSIC

Several pubs around the city have traditional nights, either organised or on an impromptu basis. A selection is given below; full details from *In Dublin* and newspapers.

Comhaltas Ceoltóirí Eireann, 32 Belgrave Sq, Monkstown, Co Dublin *Tel 800295*

Central source of information; céilis and music sessions several nights a week.
An Béal Bocht, 58 Charlemont St, 2 *Tel 755614*
The Culturlann, 32 Belgrave Sq, Monkstown, Co Dublin *Tel 800295*
The Brazen Head, Lr Bridge St, 8 *Tel 779549*
Hughes's, Chancery St, 7

Tel 746945
Kitty O'Shea's, 23 Upr Canal St, 4 *Tel 609965*
O'Donoghue's, Merrion Row, 2 *Tel 762807*
The Merchant, 12 Bridge St, 8 (off Merchant's Quay) *Tel 793797*
Purty Kitchen, Dun Laoghaire, Co Dublin *Tel 801257*
Slattery's, 129 Capel St, 2 *Tel 740416*

Shopping

South of the river has always been considered the fashionable end of Dublin, with Grafton Street at its heart; the north side, for the more budget-conscious, includes the city's main thoroughfare, O'Connell Street. Just off O'Connell Street lies Henry Street, one of the busiest and most lucrative retailing streets in Europe and focal point for north-side shoppers. The O'Connell/Henry Street area has department stores.

Lying within these shopping districts are a number of comparatively young shopping complexes. South of the river, the Powerscourt Townhouse Centre on Clarendon Street is an aesthetically pleasing, bright, relaxing, shopping complex, converted from a 200-year-old mansion and courtyard. Its Crafts and Antiques Gallery in particular is worth a long browse and the centre is a popular rendezvous.

The Royal Hibernian Way, built on the site of the lamented Hibernian Hotel on Dawson Street, has become Dublin's newest showcase for designers of glamour, elegance and wealth.

The William Elliott Centre on the site of the old Wicklow Hotel on Wicklow Street always has a few interesting tenants tucked away upstairs, including a few boutiques of note.

The Tower Design Craft Centre is part of the Industrial Development Authority's imaginative programme for industrial renewal and job creation in Dublin's inner city. Once a sugar refinery, the Tower now houses more than 35 workshops. In Rathfarnham, the Marlay Craft Courtyard is a similar enterprise, converted from a 200-year-old courtyard building, and can form the basis of a lovely day out at the foot of the Dublin Mountains.

The Ilac Centre (pronounced eye-lack) has Dunnes Stores—Ireland's largest, cheapest chain-store, where T shirts and tights, pure wool sweaters and suits can be bought at bargain basement prices. For design, finish and value,

check out middle- to up-market clothing by Irish designers in Irish linen, tweeds and wool. The work of young and talented contemporary artists may be seen and bought at bargain prices in art galleries around the city, and in the crafts category, handmade pottery and jewellery are excellent buys. Waterford Crystal prices will be the same whichever shop you choose, so shop around for choice rather than value. (Switzers' Waterford Crystal Palace stocks the entire range.) There are other brands of Irish crystal available however, and it may be worth your while comparing prices for similar pieces.

ANTIQUES

Antique shops around Dublin tend to be found in clusters; the following are good areas to try.

The Antique Gallery, Powerscourt Townhouse Centre; Bachelor's Walk, Clarendon St, Dawson St, Duke St, Francis St, Kildare St, Molesworth St, Ormond Quay, South Anne St.
Fine Arts, Antique and Furniture sales are held in various sale-rooms in the city at regular intervals. The Fine Arts section in Saturday's *Irish Times* is a good source of up-to-date information.

BOOKSELLERS

Assisi Bookshop, Merchant's Quay, 8 *Tel 770890* Religious books.
The Bookshop, Rathfarnham Shopping Centre, 14 *Tel 934733*
Books Unlimited, Northside Shopping Centre, Coolock, 5 *Tel 480066* and Unit 46, Donaghmede Shopping Centre, 13 *Tel 470952*
Books Upstairs, 25 Market Arcade, Sth Great George's St, 2 *Tel 710064*
Chapters Bookshop, 21 Wicklow St, 2 *Tel 688328*
Christian Publication Centre, 110 Middle Abbey St, 1 *Tel 726754*
Easons, 40–42 Lr O'Connell St, 1 *Tel 733811*

Eblana Bookshop, 50 Middle Abbey St, 1 *Tel 787633*
Greene & Co, 16 Clare St, 2 *Tel 762554*
New and secondhand books.
Fred Hanna Ltd 27/29 Nassau St, 2 *Tel 771255*
Hodges Figgis, 41 Dawson St, 2 *Tel 774754*
The Library Shop, Trinity College, College St, 2 *Tel 772941*
Maps, atlases and travel books.
The Paperback Centre, 20 Suffolk St, 2 *Tel 774210* and 14 Stillorgan, *Tel 886341*
Readers Digest, 18 Lr Liffey St, 1 *Tel 744100*
Waterstones Bookshop, 7 Dawson St, 2 *Tel 791415*
George Webb, 5 Crampton Quay, 1 *Tel 777489*
Book bargains; Victorian plate-books, old books of Irish interest.

CONCERT TICKETS

HMV, 18 Henry St, 1 *Tel 732899* 65 Grafton St, 2 *Tel 795332* *Tel 795364* (24 hrs) for credit card bookings
Golden Discs (see *Records & Cassettes*)

CRAFTS

See also *Bord Fáilte Information Sheet No 20.*

Crafts Council of Ireland, Thomas Prior House, 4 *Tel 680684*
General information.
Best of Irish, U17, Westbury Hotel, Harry St, 1 *Tel 791233*
The Craft Gallery, Powerscourt Townhouse Centre, 2
Dublin Crystal Glass Co, Carysfort Ave, Blackrock, Co Dublin *Tel 887932/888627*
Home Thoughts, 14 South Anne St, 2 *Tel 770479*
The Kilkenny Shop, Nassau St, 2 *Tel 777066*
Marlay Craft Courtyard, Marlay Park, Rathfarnham, 16 *Tel 942083* 200-year-old courtyard divided into workshops leased to professional craftsmen working at painting, glassware, pottery, weaving and bookbinding;

pretty tearoom and shop.

Needlecraft, 27 Dawson St, 2
Tel 772493
Wools, art, needlework and
tapestries.

O'Farrell Workshops Ltd, 62
Dawson St, 2 *Tel 770862*

This is It, U13 Irish Life Mall,
Talbot St, 1 *Tel 728551*

Tower Design Craft Centre,
Pearse St, 2 *Tel 775655*
Similar to Marlay Park.

West Wicklow Craft Shop, 16
Creation Arcade, Grafton St, 2
Tel 776488

DELICATESSENS

John Caviston, 59 Glasthule Rd,
Sandycove, Co Dublin *Tel 809120*

The Cheeseboard Ltd, Westbury
Mall, 2 *Tel 791422*

***Dunn's,** 6 Upper Baggot St, 2
Tel 602688

Fitzers, 41 Lr Camden St, 2
Tel 753996

Fothergills, 141 Upper Rathmines
Rd, 6 *Tel 962511*

Gourmet Shop, 48 Highfield Rd, 6
Tel 970365

Magills, 14 Clarendon St, 2
Tel 713830

***McConnell & Nelson,** 38
Grafton St, 2 *Tel 774344*

***Molloy's,** 47 Donnybrook Rd, 4
Tel 691678

**Denotes those which stock and mail
smoked salmon to Britain, USA and
mainland Europe.*

DEPARTMENT STORES

Arnott & Co, 12 Henry St, 1
Tel 721111

BHS (Dublin) Ltd, O'Connell St,
1 *Tel 720466*

Brown Thomas & Co, 15 Grafton
St, 2 *Tel 776861*

Clery & Co, O'Connell St, 1
Tel 786000

Dunnes Stores Ltd, Ilac Centre, 1
Tel 730211

The Kilkenny Shop, Nassau St, 2
Tel 777066

Marks & Spencer, 24 Mary St, 1
Tel 728833

Penneys, 47 Mary St, 1 *Tel 727788*

Roches' Stores, 54 Henry St, 1
Tel 730044

Switzer & Co, 92 Grafton St, 2
Tel 776821

FASHION ACCESSORIES

H Johnston Ltd, 11 Wicklow St, 2
Tel 771249

Kamouflage Ltd, 50 Dawson St, 2
Tel 777696

Ciaran Peters, Parnell Mall, Ilac
Centre, Henry St, 1 *Tel 729412*

FASHION–DESIGNERS

Michel Ambers, 98/99 Clanbrassil
St, 8 *Tel 535744*

Paul Costelloe, Brown Thomas &

Co, 15 Grafton St, 2 *Tel 776861*

Pat Crowley, 14 Duke St, 2
Tel 710219

Design Centre, Powerscourt
Townhouse Centre, 2 *Tel 795718*

Ib Jorgensen, 53 Dawson St, 2
Tel 718111

Richard Lewis, 26 South
Frederick St, 2 *Tel 606160*

Michael Mortell, Westbury
Centre, Balfe St, 2 *Tel 791600*

Quinn & Donnelly, 38 Clarendon
St, 2 *Tel 719424*

Louise Raymond, Balfe St, 2 *Tel
795250*

John Rocha, Chinatown,
Powerscourt Townhouse
Centre, 2 *Tel 791393*

Mariad Whisker, 23 Dawson St, 2
Tel 762647

Henry White, 15 South Summer
St, 8 *Tel 533611*

Thomas Wolfangel, 99 Lr Baggot
St, 2 *Tel 766547*

FASHION – WOMEN

Richard Alan & Co, 58 Grafton
St, 2 *Tel 775149*

Anastasia, Westbury Centre, 2
Tel 794511

Aquascutum, 51c Dawson St, 2
Tel 770522

Laura Ashley, 60 Grafton St, 2
Tel 795433

Pia Bang, Powerscourt
Townhouse Centre, 2 *Tel 794249*

Benetton, 81 Grafton St, 2
Tel 779877

Diana Donnelly, 16 Sandford Rd,
6 *Tel 976128*

Ebony, 71 Grafton St, 2 *Tel 774655*

Monica John, William Elliott
Centre, Wicklow St, 2 *Tel 794290*

Kenji, 80 Grafton St, 2 *Tel 774499*

Koko, William Elliott Centre,
Wicklow Street, 2 *Tel 793034*

Otokio, 3 South Anne St, 2
Tel 777325

Jenny Vander, Antique Clothing,
20 South City Market, off South
Gt George's St 2 *Tel 770406*

FASHION – MEN

Alias Tom, 2 Duke Lane, 2
Tel 777772

Michael Barrie, 20 Duke St, 2
Tel 715265

Louis Copeland, 30 Lr Pembroke
St, 2 *Tel 606235*
and 30 Capel St, 1 *Tel 721600*

Ecru High Fashion, 31 Grafton
St, 2 *Tel 774133*

F X Kelly, 48 Grafton St, 2
Tel 778211

Kennedy & McSharry, 39 Nassau
St, 2 *Tel 778770*

Kevin & Howlin Ltd, 31 Nassau
St, 2 *Tel 770257*

Savoy Taylors Guild, 47 Grafton
St, 2 *Tel 713660*

John Taylor Ltd, 35 Kildare St, 2
Tel 616007

FISHING TACKLE

ABC Angling, 15 St Mary's
Abbey, 7 *Tel 731525*

Garnetts & Keegan's, 31
Parliament St, 2 *Tel 777472*
All types of fishing gear with a
full range of Barbour coats.

Rory's Fishing Tackle, 17a
Temple Bar, 2 *Tel 772351*
Sole agents for Bruce and
Walker; expert staff.

FOOTWEAR

Shoeshops have virtually taken
over Grafton St and a good deal of
Henry St. The following are shops
that stock high-fashion or unusual
footwear:

Bertie, 32 Wicklow St, 2 *Tel 770841*

Kamouflage, The Galleria Centre,
6 St Stephen's Green, 2
Tel 777696
Exclusive stockists of Tokio
Kumagai footwear.

Natural Shoe Store, 25 Drury St,
2 *Tel 714978*

Thomas Patrick, 77 Grafton St, 2
Tel 713866
Bruno Magli Shop upstairs.

Carl Scarpa, 25 Grafton St, 2
Tel 777846

The Shoe Boutique, 22 Wicklow
St, 2 *Tel 777491*

FURNITURE

Interconnections, Furniture and
Interior Design, 7 Crowe St, 2
Tel 713867

O'Hagan Design, 99 Capel St, 1
Tel 726440

HERALDRY

Heraldic Artists Ltd, 3 Nassau St,
2 *Tel 762391*

Heraldic House, 36 Upr
O'Connell St, 1 *Tel 741133*

Thomas and Emmet O'Baoill,
Tower Design Craft Centre,
Pearse St, 2 *Tel 775655*

JEWELLERS

Patrick Flood, Goldsmith
Designer, Powerscourt
Townhouse Centre, 2 *Tel 794256*

Emma Stewart Liberty,
Powerscourt Townhouse
Centre, 2 *Tel 791603*

Tower Design Craft Centre,
Pearse St, 2 *Tel 775655*

Weir & Sons, 96 Grafton St, 2
Tel 779678

West, 33 Grafton St, 2 *Tel 777275*

LINGERIE

Susan Hunter, 13 Westbury
Centre, 2 *Tel 791271*

Un Coin de Paris, Duke Lane, 2
Tel 774525

MARKETS

Dublin Corporation Market, St
Michan's St, 7

Fruit, fish, vegetables and
flowers. Mon–Fri 7am–5pm;
Tue 7am–4pm; Sat 7.30am–
11am

Iveagh Market, Francis St, 8 Tue–
Sat 9am–6pm

Liberty Market, Meath St, 8
Clothes and household goods.
Fri and Sat

Moore Street Market, 1
Colourful fruit, flowers and
vegetable market just off Henry
St with streetside barrow
vendors. Mon–Sat 9am–6pm

MILLINERS

Paul Moreland, Powerscourt
Townhouse Centre, 2 *Tel 793832*

A C O'Reilly, 31 Wicklow St, 2
Tel 770923

RECORDS AND CASSETTES

Claddagh Records, 2 Cecilia St, 2
Tel 770262
Specialist folk shop.

Dolphin Discs Branches in Moore
St, 1, Capel St, 1, Marlboro St, 1,
Talbot St, 1 *Tel 729998*

Golden Disc Group Branches at 1

Grafton Arcade, 2, 8 North Earl
St, 1, Ilac Centre, 1, 17 Upr
Liffey St, 1 *Tel 792118*

HMV Branches at 65 Grafton St, 2
Tel 795332 and 18 Henry St, 1
Tel 732899

**International Record Lending
Library,** 17a South Anne St, 2
Tel 770327

McCullough Pigott Ltd, 11
Suffolk St, 2 *Tel 773138*

Music Maker, 4 St Mary's Abbey,
1 *Tel 730347*

Opus Two, 28 Georges St Arcade,
2 *Tel 778571*

Virgin Megastore, Aston Quay, 2
Tel 777361

Walton's Musical Galleries, 2
Nth Frederick St, 1 *Tel 747805*

SPORTS GOODS

Allweather Marine Ltd, Grand
Canal Quay (off Pearse St), 2
Tel 713655
Open 8.30am–8.30pm Mon–
Fri; 8.30am–5.30pm Sat & Sun;
364 days a year.

Arnott & Co, Henry St, 1

Tel 721111

J J Fitzgibbon, 8 Sth Anne St, 2
Tel 771433

Garnetts & Keegan's, 31
Parliament St, 2 *Tel 777472*

Great Outdoors Ltd, Chatham
Hse, Chatham St, 2 *Tel 794293*

Martial Arts Centre, Castle Hse,
Sth Gt Georges St, 2 *Tel 712164*

Scout Shop, 14 Fownes St, 2
Tel 712055

Paddy Whelan & Co, 119 Cork
St, 8 *Tel 535857*

WOOLLENS

Blarney Woollen Mills, 21/23
Nassau St, 2 *Tel 710068*

Cleo Ltd, 18 Kildare St, 2
Tel 761421

Dublin Woollen Co, Metal Bridge
Corner, 1 *Tel 770301*

Irish Cottage Industries, 44
Dawson St, 2 *Tel 713039*

The Irish Scene, Powerscourt
Townhouse Centre, 2 *Tel 794061*

Monaghan's, Grafton Arcade,
Grafton St, 2 *Tel 770823*

The Sweater Shop, 9 Wicklow St,
2 *Tel 713270*

Sports

Up-to-date information on
competitions and matches is
available in the daily papers, most
of which feature comprehensive
sports diaries at the weekends. Or
consult *In Dublin* magazine.

ANGLING

For coarse anglers, Dublin's
canals—the Royal and Grand
which connect the Shannon to
Dublin—provide good fishing
stretches not far from the city.
Year-round fishing is possible as
there is no legal closed season, but
there are 'best' times for different
species and visitors are asked to
note the conservation laws
regarding some. The position
regarding licences is under review;
at present none is required, nor are
permits—except very rarely on
private fisheries. If bringing your
own bait into Ireland, take care that
it is not packed in soil or vegetable
material, the importation of which
is prohibited by law. Competition
details are available in *Ireland
Freshwater Angling* and *Gala Angling
Festivals*—both available from
Irish Tourist offices.

Game anglers need a licence for
both salmon and sea trout fishing,
though only one is needed for
both. Licences are available from
the Central Fisheries Board,
Balnagowan House, Mobhi
Boreen, Glasnevin (*tel 379206*), the
relevant Regional Fishing Board
(see Bord Fáilte sheets below) and

from selected tackle dealers. Some
salmon fishing is free or available at
a nominal charge, but almost all sea
trout fisheries are under private or
club control. Check with the
Fisheries Board.

Sea angling is an all-year-round
sport offering huge variety,
depending on the time of year.
Recommended centres around
Dublin include Skerries, Howth
and Dun Laoghaire. Anglers are
asked to return as many fish as
possible alive to the water. The
Bord Fáilte booklet *Sea Angling in
Ireland* gives details of boats, maps,
festivals and bait and is available
from any Irish Tourist Office, or
by post from the Irish Tourist
Board Literature Dept, PO
Box 1083, Dublin 8 (*tel 747733* for
price information). *Bord Fáilte
Information Sheets Nos 41, 42 and 43*
on sea, coarse and game angling
respectively will prove useful to the
visitor.

Irish Federation of Sea Anglers:
Mr Hugh O'Rorke, Secretary, 67
Windsor Drive, Monkstown, Co
Dublin *Tel 806873*

**Irish Match Angling and
Surfcasting Association**
(IMASA): Mr Michael Dixon,
36 Ralahine, Ballybrack, Co
Dublin *Tel 854159*

BADMINTON

Badminton Hall, Whitehall Rd,
12 *Tel 508101* (office hours)
505966 (court bookings)

The Badminton Clinic, 64
Ailesbury Grove, 16 *Tel 980349*
for coaching sessions.

BEACHES

Popular sandy beaches may be
found at Dollymount (3½ miles
from Dublin), Howth (9 miles),
Sutton (7 miles), Portmarnock
(9 miles), Donabate (13 miles),
Malahide (9 miles), Sandycove
(9 miles). Lovely strands for
walking and sunbathing close to
the south city centre are at
Sandymount and Merrion.

BOARDSAILING

Boardsailing is gaining in
popularity all the time, and
although the Atlantic swells on
Ireland's west coast are hard to
beat, Dublin will still provide a
reasonable challenge for
enthusiasts, whatever their
experience. See *Bord Fáilte
Information Sheet No 35.*

Irish Boardsailing Association,
or **Irish Windsurfing Class
Association,** c/o Irish Yachting
Association, 3 Park Rd, Dun
Laoghaire, Co Dublin *Tel 800239*

Skerries Boardsailing School, 7
Convent Lane, Skerries, Co
Dublin *Tel 491734/490068* after
6.30pm

Fingall Sailing School, Upper
Strand, Broadmeadow Estuary,
Malahide, Co Dublin *Tel 451979*

Glenans Irish Sailing Centre, 28
Merrion Sq, Dublin 2 *Tel 767775/
611481*

BOWLING

There are a dozen or so clubs dotted all around the city. For information contact Mr J J Burke, Dookinelly, 13 Glenabbey Rd, Mount Merrion, Co Dublin *Tel 880255*

CANOEING

The Liffey Descent (the Irish International Marathon Canoe-Racing Championships) is held in September when 30 million tons of water are released from a reservoir into the River Liffey, turning it from a well-behaved old lady into a raging torrent.

See also *Bord Fáilte Information Sheet No 11.*

Irish Canoe Union, 4/5 Eustace St, 2 *Tel 719690*

Irish Canoe Hire, Lackenash, Barnhill Rd, Dalkey, Co Dublin *Tel 854933/844288*

GAELIC GAMES

Gaelic football and hurling are the great rural pastimes on Sunday afternoons in Ireland. Every parish has its club, some traditionally stronger than others, but inter-parish rivalry will always ensure wild enthusiasm, stunning vigour (sometimes literally), and often flashes of real brilliance.

Important matches are the All-Ireland Finals, both played in September. The National League Finals are held in May.

The Gaelic Athletic Association (GAA) is the governing body for Gaelic games in Ireland and its headquarters are in Croke Park where most important matches are played.

Gaelic Athletic Association, Croke Park, 3 *Tel 363222*

Croke Park has two stands, both considered good (if you can get tickets for them). Of the terraced areas, Hill 16 is packed with atmosphere—but can be turbulent.

GOLF

Clubs are accessible and courses are often natural beauty spots. Green fees in Ireland are usually charged on a per day rather than per round basis; they average about £7 per day, but can go as high as £20 for some of the top championship courses. Availability of caddies (without prior arrangement) or golf cars is negligible so visitors are advised to bring only a light 'Sunday' bag as they will probably have to carry it themselves.

Although the offending clause has now been deleted from the Constitution of the Irish Golfing Union, women may only be second-class—specifically associate—members of many Irish golf clubs. This means lower membership fees but it also means fairly severe restrictions on playing times. It may be wise to check this out before heading off for your chosen course.

The Visitors' Guide to Irish Golf Courses in the Republic of Ireland lists golf courses and gives information on facilities available to visitors. See also *Bord Fáilte Information Sheet No 38.*

Golfing Union of Ireland, 81 Eglinton Road, 4 *Tel 694111*

Senior Marketing Executive—Golf, Bord Fáilte, Baggot St Bridge, 2

GYMS AND EXERCISE CENTRES

City Gym, Eden Quay, 1 *Tel 788100*

Body Klinic, 96 Pembroke Rd, 4 *Tel 607650*

Chambers, 6/7 Balfe St, 2 *Tel 773232*

Pineapple Ireland, Swanville Place, Rere 185 Lr Rathmines Rd, 6 *Tel 960967*

Litton Lane Dance Studios, 2 Litton Lane, 1 *Tel 728044*

Trimdown, 53 Middle Abbey St, 1 *Tel 723080*

Slender Health Studios, 6 Lr Kilmacud Rd Lower, Stillorgan, Co Dublin, *Tel 886871*

Squash Ireland Ltd (see *Squash* for addresses and telephone numbers)

HILL WALKING AND ROCK CLIMBING

One of the five great roads radiating from Tara in ancient Ireland was the Slí Cualann, the Wicklow Way, so called because it crosses part of the former land of Cuala, now Wicklow. The start of the Wicklow Way is served by Dublin City buses.

It follows sheep tracks, forest firebreaks and old bog roads across miles of beautiful open country; there are magnificent views. Much of it lies above 500m where sudden and drastic weather changes can occur; maps and compasses are advisable, and it is not recommended for solitary rambling.

The strong walker could cover all 126km of the Wicklow Way, but there are several shorter walks for the less energetic or those with only a few hours to spare.

Further information from *Bord Fáilte Information Sheet No 30; The Wicklow Guide* (Bord Fáilte); *The Open Road* and *Walking in Wicklow* by J B Malone.

HORSE RACING

Racing is one of the great Irish sports. Two top class tracks lie only a few miles south and north of the city centre—Leopardstown and the Phoenix Park respectively.

Big days in the Irish racing calendar include: the Airlie/Coolmore Irish 2000 Guineas (May); Goffs Irish 1000 Guineas (May); the Budweiser Irish Derby (June)—the most glamorous outing of the year; the Gilltown Stud Irish Oaks (July); and the Jefferson Smurfit Memorial Irish St Leger (October). These are all held at the Curragh in Co Kildare.

Favourite tracks for National Hunt followers include Leopardstown; Fairyhouse, Co Meath (where the Irish Grand National is held on Easter Monday); Punchestown (famous for its three-day Festival meeting in late April); and Navan (feature race the Troytown Chase). All lie within an hour's drive of Dublin.

Racegoers in Ireland can place their bets either with the course bookmakers or with the Tote. The Tote pays according to the official starting price regardless of when the bet is placed. It also offers combination bets and a jackpot.

All the Irish national newspapers carry details of the day's race-meetings and carry results on the following day. Other publications include: *Irish Racing Annual* (ed Smith and McGinty): published in early December, it reviews the previous 12 months of home and international racing; *Guide to Irish Racing* (ed Wall): published end of March, this gives predictions for the year ahead for Flat and National Hunt racing in Ireland; *Bord Fáilte Information Sheet No 54.*

HORSE RIDING

Hacking and trekking are offered by many schools in easy reach of Dublin. See *Bord Fáilte Information Sheet No 65.*

Bord nag Capall, Irish Horse Board, Irish Farm Centre, Naas Rd, 12 *Tel 501166*

ICE SKATING

Dublin Ice Rink, Dolphin's Barn, 8 *Tel 532170*

Silver Skate Ice Rink, 376 North Circular Rd, 7 *Tel 301263*

ROWING

The major regatta in Ireland is the Dublin Metropolitan Regatta, held on a straight, 6-laned, 2000 metre course, as required by FISA for International Regattas. The programme is finalised in

November; contact Bord Fáilte or the IARU. Islandbridge, the headquarters of most Dublin rowing clubs, is on a point of the River Liffey ideally suited for the sport. Contact Mary F McGrath, Hon Secretary, IARU, 5 Ardee Road, Rathmines, 6 *Tel 962608*. See also *Bord Fáilte Information Sheet No 15*.

RUGBY UNION

Landsdowne Road is the headquarters of Irish rugby, and is also the venue for all matches played in the Five Nations Championship, including the Triple Crown. These matches are played during January, February and March, and stand-tickets for home games can be rare.

Landsdowne Road has 22,000 stand-seats divided between stands on both sides of the pitch. Terracing at both ends is adequate but distinctly uncomfortable if it rains (umbrellas will be discouraged by the more vocal behind you) or if conditions become very crowded.

There is a lively club rugby scene around the city. For details see daily newspapers or contact: Irish Rugby Football Union, 62 Landsdowne Rd, 4 *Tel 684601*

SAILING

The oldest Yacht Club in the world is Irish—the Royal Cork Yacht Club, which celebrated its 250th anniversary in 1970. Dublin has some venerable clubs of her own, however, including the National Yacht Club, the Royal Irish Yacht Club, the Royal St George Yacht Club and the Dun Laoghaire Motor Yacht Club, all situated in Dun Laoghaire. Howth Harbour also has a lively club, and there are several areas along the coastline where dinghy sailing as well as keelboat sailing are popular.

Yachts or dinghies may be brought into Ireland for a temporary period without liability for tax or duty. Owners of sea-

going yachts must apply to the harbour masters of all ports in which they wish to anchor. On arrival at the first port of entry, the flag 'Q' should be shown. Contact should then be made with the Customs and Excise Officer or with a Garda. Irish laws on the importation of cats and dogs are extremely restrictive (except from Britain); a licence must be obtained beforehand from the Dept of Agriculture, Dublin 2. Further information from the Irish Yachting Association, 3 Park Rd, Dun Laoghaire, Co Dublin *Tel 800239*

A full-time secretariat is available to give further information to visiting yachtsmen. See also *Bord Fáilte Information Sheet No 28*.

SOCCER

Soccer in Ireland consists mainly of the League of Ireland and occasional international or representative matches. The Irish RFU's ground at Landsdowne Road is the usual venue for big international soccer matches. Less important competitions take place at Dalymount and Tolka Parks on the north side of the city.

League of Ireland matches are played every Sunday afternoon during the season on various grounds around the city. For details see national newspapers or contact: **The Football Association of Ireland,** 80 Merrion Sq South, 2 *Tel 766864*

SQUASH

Squash Ireland Ltd Branches at:
Clontarf (*Tel 331656*)
Dalkey (*801515*)
Dartry (*963910*)
Phoenix Park (*385850*)
Visitors' fees include full gymnasium facilities, sauna, etc.

SWIMMING BATHS

There is an admission charge to these pools. Telephone individual pools for opening hours.

Ballyfermot, Le Fanu Park, 10
  Tel 266504
Ballymun, Ballymun Shopping
  Centre, 10 *Tel 421368*
Coolock, Coolock Shopping
  Centre, 5 *Tel 477743*
Crumlin, Windmill Rd, 12
  Tel 555792
Finglas, Mellowes Rd, 11
  Tel 348005
Townsend St, Linn Snahma
  Markievicz, 2 *Tel 770503*
Rathmines, Williams Park,
  Rathmines, 6 *Tel 961275*
Sean McDermott St, 1
  Tel 720752

OUTSIDE DUBLIN

**Monkstown Indoor Heated
  Pool,** Monkstown, Co Dublin
  Tel 807100
  Admission charge
Dun Laoghaire
  Open Sea Baths *Tel 806965*
Blackrock
  Open Sea Baths *Tel 888306*

TENNIS

This is a selection of public courts. Further information from Irish Lawn Tennis Association, 22 Upr Fitzwilliam St, 2 *Tel 606332*

Bushy Park, Terenure, 6
  Tel 900320
Herbert Park, Ballsbridge, 4
  Tel 684364
Orwell Quarry (behind Terenure
  Village), 6
St Anne's Estate, Dollymount, 3
  Tel 313697

WATER-SKIING

Irish Water-Ski Association,
  7 Upper Beaumont Drive,
  Ballintemple, Cork
  Tel (021) 292411
Golden Falls Water-Ski Club,
  Ballymore Eustace, Co Kildare offers facilities to non-club members. For details contact Des Burke-Kennedy, Mount Salus, Knocknaree, Dalkey, Co Dublin *Tel 855205*

Transport

Dublin is a small, compact city with most of its attractions lying conveniently within a one-mile radius, and many will tell you that the only way to see it is on foot. Because of its one-way street system and a dearth of good signposting, it is not recommended territory for visiting car drivers. You are therefore advised to find a secure car park, leave the car, and choose between walking, finding a bus or taking a taxi.

BUSES

Dublin's public bus service is

regular and comparatively cheap crossing city and suburbs from around 6.30am on weekdays (9.30am on Sundays) to 11.30pm. 'An Lar' written on the front of a bus means The Centre.

Information on all public transport services may be obtained by telephoning *787777* (9am–9pm weekdays, Sundays 10am–7pm). Bus Éireann (the Dublin City Bus Service) also runs day tours both around the city and to outlying areas. They start from the Central Bus Station (Busáras), Store St, Dublin 1, and tickets are available

only from there if purchased on day of travel. Otherwise, the tourist offices at 14 and 59 Upper O'Connell St, or American Express, 116 Grafton St, Dublin 2 will also take bookings.

SUBURBAN TRAINS

Dart (the Dublin Rapid Transit System) is Iarnród Éireann's high-frequency electric rail service extending from Bray, all around Dublin Bay, up to Howth in the north of the city. Starting at 7am and continuing to midnight, trains run about every 15 minutes or so:

DIRECTORY

a pleasant way to get an overview of Dublin Bay and the suburbs.

TAXIS

Telephone a taxi (see under 'Taxi-Cab Ranks and Shelters' in the telephone directory), telephone a taxi company, find a taxi rank (see below) or try hailing a passing cab (almost impossible at peak hours). Standards vary from cigarette-infested to spotless (they are improving rapidly). Fares are metered and are subject to a minimum charge within a 10-mile radius of the city centre, plus an extra charge for each passenger, a baggage charge and a night surcharge. Tips run to about 10 per cent. Fares for journeys outside the city centre may be negotiated

directly with the driver.

City taxi ranks

Amiens St, 1; Aston's Quay, 1; Burlington Hotel, 4; College Green, 2; Eccles St, 7; Eden Quay, 1; Landsdowne Rd, 4 (near Jury's Hotel); O'Connell Street, Upper and Lower, 1; St Stephen's Green, 2; Westland Row station 2; 14a Wexford St, 2

CAR HIRE

See *Bord Fáilte Information Sheet No 21* for a list of companies who are members of the Car Rental Council, and operate according to a Code of Standards drawn up by them and Bord Fáilte. They include:

Avis Rent-a-Car Ltd, 1 Hanover St East, 2 *Tel 776971*
Boland's Car Hire Rentals, 38 Pearse St, 2 *Tel 770704*
Hertz Rent-a-Car, 19/20 Hogan Place, Lr Grand Canal St, 2 *Tel 767476*
Murrays Europcar Rent-a-Car, Baggot St Bridge, 4 *Tel 681777*

CAR PARKS

There are over a dozen controlled car parks around the city centre, including those at: Setanta Place, 2; Drury St, 2; Marlborough St, 1; Ilac Centre, 1.

HORSE-DRAWN CABS

Restored horse-drawn cabs may be hired from Paddy Sarsfield, 5 Lr Kevin St, 8 *Tel 755995*

Useful Information

AUTOMOBILE ASSOCIATION

AA Centre, 23 Suffolk St, 2 *Tel 779481*
Mon–Fri 9am–5pm, Sat 9am–12.30pm.

BANKS

From Monday to Friday banks are open from 10am to 12.30, and from 1.30 to 3pm (except Thursday when they remain open until 5pm). Closed Saturday, Sunday and Bank Holidays. Dublin Airport Bank is the exception, remaining open every day (except Christmas Day) from 7.30am–11pm; from October to March, 8.30am–9.30pm.

Allied Irish Banks and Bank of Ireland, the two main banking groups in Ireland, have branches all over Dublin; those in the city centre include:

AIB
64 Grafton St, 2 *Tel 773584*
100 Grafton St, 2 *Tel 713011*
7 Dame St, 2 *Tel 793211*
10 Lr O'Connell St, 2 *Tel 730555*
63 Upr O'Connell St, 2 *Tel 731500*
Group Headquarters, Bankcentre, Ballsbridge, 4 *Tel 600311*
Bank of Ireland
Airport *Tel 420433*
2 College Green, 2 *Tel 776801*
6 Lr O'Connell St, 1 *Tel 729799*
39 St Stephen's Green East, 2 *Tel 761976*
1 Westmoreland St, 1 *Tel 776801*
Group Headquarters, Lr Baggot St, 2 *Tel 615933*
Bank of America, Russell Court, St Stephen's Green, 2 *Tel 781222*

Bank of Nova Scotia, 65 St Stephen's Green, 2 *Tel 781388*
Barclays Bank, 47 St Stephen's Green, 2 *Tel 613688*
Northern Bank, 27 College Green, 2 (Agents for Midland) *Tel 798788*
Ulster Bank Ltd, 33 College Green, 2 (Agents for Nat West) *Tel 777623*
Algemene Bank Nederland, 121 St Stephen's Green, 2 *Tel 717333*
First National Bank of Chicago, 44 St Stephen's Green, 2 *Tel 681522*
Banque Nationale de Paris, 111 St Stephen's Green West, 2 *Tel 712811*
Chase Bank Ltd, 18 St Stephen's Green North, 2 *Tel 785111*

BUREAUX DE CHANGE

Most banks have facilities for cashing travellers' cheques and exchanging currency. Travellers' cheques are accepted by most hotels, large shops, transport and travel companies. Facilities are also provided by:

Dublin & East Tourism, 14 Upr O'Connell St, 1 *Tel 747733*
Thomas Cook, 118 Grafton St, 2 *Tel 771721/771307*
American Express, 116 Grafton St, 2 *Tel 772874*

CHEMISTS (Late Night)

O'Connell Pharmacy, 55 Lr O'Connell St, 1 *Tel 730427*
310 Harold's Cross Road, 6 *Tel 973977*
Open 7 days until 10pm

DOCTORS AND DENTISTS

For a list of doctors and dentists, see the *Golden Pages* telephone directory.

Irish Medical Organisation, 10 Fitzwilliam Place, 2 *Tel 767273*
Irish Dental Association, 29 Kenilworth Square, 6 *Tel 978435*

ELECTRICITY

220 volts/50 cycles is usual in Ireland. Many hotels have 220/110 volt plugs for shavers.

EMERGENCIES

In life-threatening emergencies, telephone 999 from any call-box and say which service is required—Fire Brigade, Police or Ambulance. There is no charge for the call. See also *Hospitals* below.

GENEALOGY

See *Bord Fáilte Information Sheet No 8, Tracing Your Ancestors.*
Hibernian Research, Windsor House, 22 Windsor Rd, 6 *Tel 966522* (24 hours)
Genealogical Office, Kildare St, 2 *Tel 765521*

GUIDES

Dublin & East Tourism, 14 Upr O'Connell St, 2 *Tel 747733*
Grayline Dublin City Tours, 14 O'Connell St, 2 *Tel 744466*
Bus Éireann, c/o Dublin & East Tourism, or **Central Bus Station** (Busaras), 35 Lr Abbey St, 1 *Tel 300777* or (callers only) 59 Upr O'Connell St, 1

HEALTH

Visitors from another EEC country

If a visitor to Ireland from another EEC country is eligible under EEC Social Security Regulations (ie if they are insured workers), they and their dependants, if they are on a short visit (eg holidays or a business trip) can receive urgent medical care for sudden sickness or accident in the same way as an Irish national who holds a medical card. For list of doctors contact Eastern Health Board, Emmet House, 138/140 Thomas St, 8 *Tel 719222*. Hours 9am–5pm Monday–Friday.

It is necessary for visitors from EEC countries other than UK to present Form E111 when visiting a doctor on contract or hospital. Visitors from the UK need only give their UK address and their national insurance number to the doctor on contract from whom they are seeking treatment. Further details from the Chief Executive Officer, Eastern Health Board, 1 James's St, 8 *Tel 537951* or from local Health Centres.

Visitors from non-EEC countries

You can obtain health services as above, but will have to pay (depending on your insurance arrangements).

Urgent medical treatment

Emergency medical services are available 24 hours a day. Ring any of the hospitals below to find out which ones are 'on call'. Or telephone 999 for an ambulance.

HOSPITALS

Jervis Street Hospital, Jervis St, 1 *Tel 723355*
Mater Misericordiae, Eccles St, 7 *Tel 301122*
National Maternity Hospital, Holles St, 2 *Tel 608788*
Rotunda Maternity Hospital, Parnell Sq, 1 *Tel 730700*
St James's, James's St, 8 *Tel 537941*
St Vincent's, Elm Park, 4 *Tel 694533*

LOOS

The average Dubliner will not resort to a public convenience if he or she can help it, preferring to find a convenient pub, restaurant or hotel. Pubs are probably the best bet (except during the 'Holy Hour' when they are legally obliged to close between 2.30 and 3.30pm), as they don't have doors that demand a 5p piece when you are least likely to have it. Department stores (Arnotts, Clery's, Brown Thomas, Switzers) all have loos but usually have endless queues as well. There is a public convenience in the city centre in the 'triangle' between Trinity College and Westmoreland Street.

NEWSAGENTS/NEWSPAPERS

Daily papers include:
Cork Examiner, 95 Patrick St, Cork *Tel (021) 963300* and 7 Aston Quay, 2 *Tel 770791*
Irish Independent, Independent House, 90 Middle Abbey St, 1 *Tel 731666*
Irish Press, Burgh Quay, 2 *Tel 713333*
Irish Times, D'Olier St, 2 *Tel 792022*

Foreign newspapers are available from:
Bus Stop, Gaiety Corner, 52 Grafton St, 2 *Tel 773661*
Eason & Son, 40/42 Lr O'Connell St, 1 *Tel 733811*

OPTICIANS

See *Golden Pages* telephone directory. For emergency repairs:
Dublin Pharmacy Ltd, 29 Westmoreland St, 2 *Tel 778698*

PHOTOGRAPHY

Most pharmacies sell and develop film. For speedy print developing, there are several one-hour shops around the city, including:
Fujicolor Service Centre, 148 Lr Baggot St, 2 *Tel 789644*
One Hour Photo, 110 Grafton St, 2 *Tel 774472*

POST OFFICES

Central post offices such as those at St Andrew St (off Wicklow St) and South Anne St (off Grafton St) are open from 9am–5.30pm on weekdays only. The General Post Office (GPO), O'Connell Street, *Tel 728888* is open 8am–8pm on weekdays, and on Sundays and Bank Hols from 10.30am–6pm.

TELEPHONES

Ireland's telephones were famously bad but have improved dramatically. The public telephones called 'Payphones' enable a caller to dial local, trunk and international calls direct. Payphones accept 5p, 10p and 50p coins. The General Post Office, O'Connell St, also has international telephoning facilities. For help with other public and private telephones, the operator can be reached by dialling 10.

TELEVISION & RADIO

Radio Telefis Éireann, Donnybrook, Dublin 4, (*Tel 693111*) operates the state-run radio and television system. The BBC, British Independents and Channel 4 are also picked up along the east coast together with a number of satellite channels.
Radio 1 *88.5 MHz*
News, shows, light music.
Radio 2 *90.7 MHz*
Pop music.
Radio na Gaeltachta *92.9 MHz*
Irish language channel.

FM3 *92.9 MHz*
Classical music (afternoons – shared channel).

TIPPING

Where tips are given, they can be in the order of 10–15 per cent, for instance to taxi drivers, hairdressers, barbers, and waiting staff in hotels and restaurants. Some hotels and restaurants incorporate a service charge which should find its way to staff.

When paying in pubs, if the service has been particularly pleasant or helpful, a customer might offer to buy the barman or barmaid a drink. Hotel porters expect a tip of around 50p a bag, and official car park attendants usually get the same.

TOURIST INFORMATION

Information is available from Irish tourist offices dotted all over the country. The knowledge of the staff is backed up by masses of maps, guides, books and leaflets, many of which are free or available at a nominal charge. A Room Reservation Service (for personal callers) will book visitors into Bord Fáilte (Irish Tourist Board) approved premises for a small fee. The office at O'Connell Street also has Bureau de Change facilities.

Dublin & East Tourism, 14 Upr O'Connell St, 1 *Tel 747733* (Open all year round)
Dublin Airport *Tel 376387* (Open all year round)
Bord Fáilte, Baggot St, 2 *Tel 747733/765871* (Open 3 March–October)

ANNUAL EVENTS IN DUBLIN

March
Feis Ceoil
St Patrick's Day Parade
April
Dublin Grand Opera Society Spring Season
May
Spring Show and Industries Fair
June
Classical Music Festival in Great Irish Houses
Dublin Street Carnival
July
Carrolls Irish Open Golf Championships
August
Dublin Horse Show, RDS
Irish Antique Dealers Fair
September
All-Ireland Football and Hurling Finals
Dublin Theatre Festival
October
Dublin City Marathon
November
Dublin Film Festival
Irish National Stamp Exhibition
December
Dublin Grand Opera Society Winter Season

Main entries are shown in **bold**

Acknowledgements

ALL THE PHOTOGRAPHS EXCEPT THOSE LISTED BELOW WERE ESPECIALLY COMMISSIONED BY THE AA FOR THIS PUBLICATION AND TAKEN BY THE SLIDE FILE, DUBLIN.

The Automobile Association also wishes to thank the following photographers, libraries and organisations for their assistance:

Bord Fáilte 22 Young musician, Tin whistle, 23 Concertina, 77 Royal Hospital, 83 Newgrange, 92 Malahide, 95 Joyce Museum; *The Board of Trinity College Dublin* 50 Book of Kells; *Hugh Doran* 14 Belvedere House; *T Kelly* 5 Street lamp, 12 Letterbox, Dominick St, 13 Dominick St, 40 Four Courts 41 GPO Monument, 42/3 Grand Canal, 45 Mansion House, 51 Olympia Theatre, O'Connell Monument, 57 Horse Show, 61 St Patrick's, 69 Jim Larkin, 70 River Liffey, 71 Sunlight Chambers, 76 Antiques, 85 Glendalough Round Tower, 86 Howth, 89 Skerries, 90 Trim, 91 Grand Canal, 93 Howth, 104 Guinness sign; *The Mansell Collection* 9 C A Parnell, 16 Gulliver's Travels, 17 Oliver Goldsmith, Deserted Village, 18 Thomas Moore, 19 Oscar Wilde; *Mary Evans Picture Library* 8/9 Dublin, 9 Uprising; *National Gallery of Ireland* 18 James Joyce, 19 W B Yeats, 38 Custom House, 48/9 Women in the Garden; *National Library of Ireland* 10 Parliament House; *National Museum of Ireland* 50 Ardagh Chalice, Cross of Cong, Tara Brooch, 21 Harp; *Slide File* 7 Doorway, 22 Traditional Music, 23 Folk Museum, 31 Statue in the Liberties 67 Halfpenny Bridge, 79 St Patrick's, 94 Powerscourt Waterfall, Vartry Reservoir.